African-Ame

Civil Rights in the USA

David McGill

Advanced
Topic*Master*

Acknowledgements
My thanks got to Theo Schulte and Nicolas Kinloch for their advice on the content and structure of this book.

Philip Allan Updates, an imprint of Hodder Education, an Hachette UK company, Market Place, Deddington, Oxfordshire OX15 0SE

Orders
Bookpoint Ltd, 130 Milton Park, Abingdon, Oxfordshire OX14 4SB
tel: 01235 827720
fax: 01235 400454
e-mail: uk.orders@bookpoint.co.uk
Lines are open 9.00 a.m.–5.00 p.m., Monday to Saturday, with a 24-hour message answering service. You can also order through the Philip Allan Updates website: www.philipallan.co.uk

© Philip Allan Updates 2009

ISBN 978-0-340-97463-6

Impression number 5 4 3 2 1

Year 2013 2012 2011 2010 2009

Cover photograph reproduced by permission of Fotolia

Printed in Spain

Hachette UK's policy is to use papers that are natural, renewable and recyclable products and made from wood grown in sustainable forests. The logging and manufacturing processes are expected to conform to the environmental regulations of the country of origin.

P01463

Contents

Introduction

Barack Obama's victory in the US presidential elections on 4 November 2008 was seen by many as a long-awaited triumph: a triumph not just for the Democratic Party but also for African-Americans and the civil rights movement. His acceptance speech on 5 November reflected an awareness that there were many precursors to this moment, and that generations of Americans had fought for equality. It was also a patriotic speech, full of optimism and positive sentiment about America, the 'land of the free'. As he remarked:

> If there is anyone out there who still doubts that America is a place where all things are possible; who still wonders if the dream of our founders is alive in our time; who still questions the power of our democracy, tonight is your answer.

Obama highlighted the central paradox of the civil rights movement: that in a country that denied them equality African-Americans were able to use that nation's core ideas to achieve freedom. Eventually they too would be able to partake in the dream of the nation's founders. To move from slavery to citizens, all they had to do was hold their fellow Americans to the promise embodied in their own constitution that 'all men were created equal'. Not that doing this would be easy. It would take centuries before the descendants of those brought in chains to America would be able to cast their votes. But the fact that all they were doing was asking for the rights that their fellow citizens took for granted meant that in the end they were likely to achieve victory.

The election of Obama to the presidency was a significant milestone. However, it should not give a false air of inevitability to the victory hard won by civil rights campaigners over the last century. Fewer than 50 years before, Obama would not have been served in many southern restaurants and would certainly have been denied the right to vote.

This study focuses on the struggle of African-Americans to achieve equality over the last 150 years. It begins by looking at the 'standard' views of the civil rights movement and some common misconceptions. In Chapter 2 it uncovers the background to the civil rights movement and explores how the southern states constructed a segregated society that disenfranchised African-Americans. Chapter 3 examines the role the two world wars played in transforming the context of the civil rights movement, as well as the emergence of the first organisations to challenge segregation in the South. Chapters 4 and 5 look at the challenges the movement mounted to segregation. Chapter 6 outlines the success of the civil rights movement between 1963 and 1965, after it had mounted large campaigns of civil disobedience in southern cities. By the end of 1965 the South had been forced to integrate and to remove the legal obstacles to voting, education and employment that it had enforced since the 1860s. Finally, Chapter 7 looks at the legacy of the civil rights movement and what has been achieved since 1965.

The term 'blacks' is used throughout this book and is in no way intended to be derogatory. Terms defined in the glossary are highlighted in purple the first time they appear in each chapter, for easy reference.

David McGill

What are the standard views on the civil rights movement?

The 'standard' views of the civil rights movement focus on the period from 1955 to 1965, and in particular on the struggle of African-Americans to achieve full equality in the southern states of America. The civil rights movement defined in this way has a clear beginning, middle and end, and takes place at a time of intense change. The civil rights movement thus defined remains a popular subject of study both at school and college level and has been absorbed into the history of America as a tale of freedom and hope. The African-Americans' 'long walk to freedom' ends with them securing the constitutional rights of their fellow Americans.

This version of the civil rights struggle acknowledges that it is a story of injustice (after all, it took them until 1965 to secure the rights given to their fellow citizens in 1787), but it is nonetheless a story of injustice corrected. The standard view of the movement also links it to a general liberalisation of America that took place in this period. It is often studied alongside the 'counter-culture' and women's rights movements and can link into studies of the war in Vietnam and the 'hippy' movement. The success of black Americans in securing their freedoms was part of a general movement in which individual rights were fought for and won. It is a story with its heroes, such as Martin Luther King, and its villains, such as 'Bull' Connor. It is also a story in which those fighting for freedom were generally peaceful and committed to the philosophy of non-violence. Such a view of the civil rights movement emphasises its heroic qualities. Those struggling for civil rights are imbued with a sense of nobility and some have become iconic figures in modern America.

The standard story of the civil rights movement emphasises the role of those groups and individuals who fought for their freedoms. The sit-in students, the freedom riders and those who marched from Selma to Montgomery are all given prominent roles in the story. It is acknowledged that the federal government played a role, but it is seen as an often reluctant participant which got involved in settling matters when forced to do so.

The protagonists in the story are the activists, such as Martin Luther King. Under their leadership, by 1965 African-Americans had largely gained their civil rights, and the story essentially came to an end. Civil rights activists who fit less neatly into the picture are often excluded. For a time Malcolm X was such a figure. The black Americans who rioted in 1965 and 1968 (and thereafter) also barely feature in this story. In the standard view of the civil rights movement the Montgomery bus boycott of 1954–55 is not connected to the anarchy of the Watts riots of 1965 or the explosion of gang culture and violence of the 1980s. What happens after 1965 is seen as separate from what went before, and the links between the North and the South are overlooked. The treatment of blacks in the North is often dealt with in only a cursory manner. Moreover, the complexity of events and their links to Cold War politics and later economic issues are often ignored. The role of the federal government, divisions within the civil rights movement and the treatment of blacks in the North are all glossed over or dealt with in a superficial manner.

While this view of the civil rights movement contains elements of truth, it is both simplistic and overly triumphalist. Many blacks living in America today would argue that they face huge problems that both the Civil Rights Act of 1964 and the Voting Rights Act of 1965 have failed to address. Ghettoisation, 'white flight' and unemployment are contemporary issues that still limit and damage black opportunities. The structure of the judicial system and the treatment blacks face when compared with whites are also issues that continue to raise fundamental questions about race in America. However, the importance of figures such as Colin Powell and Condoleezza Rice in the Bush administration, and the electoral victory of Barack Obama, prove that change has occurred. The story of the civil rights movement needs to address all these issues and concerns and still construct a convincing narrative of events that will explain the key issues and events to students.

The standard narrative tends, after providing some contextual background, to start in 1954 with *Brown* v *Board of Education of Topeka* and end in 1965 with the Voting Rights Act. This narrative is therefore quite short, lasting roughly a decade. It focuses on the South, and on key individuals such as Martin Luther King and central organisations such as the Student Nonviolent Coordinating Committee (SNCC) and the National Association for the Advancement of Colored People (NAACP). It tends to view the civil rights movement as a political one and downplays the strong religious elements of the struggle. It therefore secularises the civil rights struggle, taking it out of the Baptist churches and into the streets and mass meetings in Washington and other cities.

The standard view of the civil rights movement underplays the role of economics and the federal government in securing equality for blacks. It must be remembered that the 1950s and 1960s were a period of modernisation for the South, in which many industries and businesses integrated without much fuss. The standard view also regards the civil rights movement as over by 1965. It ignores the continued economic inequality and endemic racism that characterised life for African-Americans in much of the North. This view also tends to ignore the Cold War context in which the struggle for civil rights was taking place. The fact that the USA was fighting an undeclared war against the USSR, one framed by the whole issue of 'freedom', is often seen as marginal, whereas in fact it was very significant.

It is important to be aware that this 'standard view' was constructed after the events occurred. The civil rights story, like all important historical events, has been 'spun'. Some of those writing about the civil rights struggle have their own agenda, and the desire to simplify it into a neat tale about the triumph of individual liberty has been strong. The civil rights movement in this context becomes another part of the 'American Dream', the enduring idea that anyone can make it against the odds to become a success story. This 'standard' view outlined above and other preconceptions about the movement can hinder full understanding of the topic. Common views taken by many students may not be complete. These views are summarised under the broad headings below, although it should be noted that there can be a degree of interplay between them.

The civil rights movement was just about African-Americans

Unfortunately, in this book this assumption is, if anything, reinforced rather than corrected. However, this is due to the constraints of space and time rather than to deliberate intent. The key point to remember is that many groups have struggled for equality throughout modern American history. Native Americans have suffered the most since the arrival of European colonists from the fifteenth century onwards. Their populations have been vastly reduced by disease and conflict and they have lost most of their lands. They have been confined to remote reservations and their communities have been ravaged by alcoholism and lack of opportunity. They have been subjected to discrimination in employment and education, and their cultures have effectively been destroyed. Their fate has been near-extinction.

Other ethnic groups that have faced challenges to their integration have included successive waves of immigrants, in particular Chinese and Japanese people. The Second World War saw much of the Japanese-American (Nisei) population interned in camps in remote areas. Many suffered a consequent loss of livelihood and educational and employment opportunities. Irish and eastern European immigrants faced discrimination after their arrival on a large scale in the nineteenth century. In recent years Hispanic immigrants have also struggled to gain equal opportunities. Commentators on America often note that it is a racially divided society. Ethnic origin is still an important determining factor in potential success in later life.

Some groups have been denied opportunities on grounds other than race, the most significant of which is arguably women. They have routinely been denied the right to have the same opportunities as men and have had to campaign hard to secure equal pay and employment rights. Since the 1960s homosexuals have also campaigned for full legal acceptance and for the right to marry, raise children and be treated fairly by the law. Religion too has been a reason for blocked opportunities: Jews have been discriminated against and Catholics have faced violence and a lack of opportunities.

There are plenty of examples of particular groups in America struggling to gain equal rights and opportunities. However, this book argues that the case of African-Americans is special in that a whole system of legal and judicial constraints was created specifically to deny them basic civil rights. The system of segregation in the South was aimed at blacks and for generations succeeded in locking them out of any chance of full participation in public life. Colour was the defining criterion and it was blacks who were targeted. This was not just racism but segregation, similar to the apartheid system created in South Africa from the 1940s. The discrimination experienced by the blacks was different from that of other groups because of its overt nature. The only group that has faced comparable attack by those in power are the Native Americans, who in many instances faced a policy of physical extermination. They were deprived of their land, their liberty and often their lives in a wholesale assault over centuries. The tribes that remain are now small in number and isolated, and it is unlikely they will ever be able to gain appropriate recompense for everything they have suffered. However, in modern times they have not been specifically targeted with legislation aimed at stopping them attending the same schools, travelling on the same buses and eating in the same restaurants as white people.

The purpose of this book is not to become involved in a complex debate about which ethnic or minority group has had the worst time or suffered the most discrimination, but to concentrate on the civil rights movement. This movement focused on securing African-Americans the same rights as their fellow citizens — particularly in the South. You simply need to be aware that the story of civil rights in America is not as simple as this suggests, and that there were other groups involved.

African-Americans were united

It is a common student mistake to assume that all African-Americans were united and motivated by the same desires. When approaching the problem, many students tend to see black Americans as a single group fighting for their rights against an oppressive white superstructure. This viewpoint ignores the significant divisions in the black community. First, there were clear differences between the key individuals, such as Martin Luther King and Malcolm X. Second, there were significant regional differences between the South and the North and between urban and regional areas. Third, there were major class divisions within the black community and religious divisions within the movement. The viewpoint of leading labour union organisers such as Philip Randolph was very different from that of religious leaders such as Martin Luther King. A homosexual ex-Communist activist such as Bayard Rustin had little in common with the leadership of the southern Baptist churches. Even so, they were capable of working together for at least some of the period.

The case of Jesse Jackson illustrates this. Jackson was born in poverty in South Carolina in 1941 and had a tough upbringing in the segregated South of the time. He won a football scholarship to the University of Illinois but dropped out and ended up back in the South in Greensboro just as the sit-in movement was starting. Initially he avoided getting caught up in civil rights issues but by 1962 he had become the leader of the Greensboro movement. In 1965 he was involved in the Selma campaign and met Martin Luther King. Soon he was involved in the Southern Christian Leadership Conference (SCLC). However, he soon left this and set up his own organisation, People United to Serve Humanity (PUSH), which linked to the broader Rainbow Coalition. He fell out with King's widow Coretta Scott King and with Andrew Young, a senior figure in King's organisation, soon after King's assassination. They refused to support Jackson's campaigns for the Democratic candidacy in the 1980s, a move that significantly weakened his credibility. He nevertheless became an established political leader over the following decades, even though many distrusted him. PUSH's headquarters on the south side of Chicago became the focus for many African-Americans' hopes for a black president.

Jackson missed his moment but his presence in American politics, though often divisive, has been important. It has also demonstrated that not all blacks in America are chasing the same dream and that divisions can be as deep and bitter as in any other coalition of interests. Louis Farrakhan, leader of the religious movement known as the Nation of Islam, exemplifies the divisions within the black community even more starkly. Many find his views extreme, but he is best known for his consistent espousal of the cause of Black Nationalism. The Nation of Islam argues that equality in America is impossible, so it would rather have separation. It is a radical viewpoint but far from original. The northern cities of America provide most support for the Nation of Islam.

Farrakhan has remained a controversial figure. Accused of anti-Semitism, he has been banned from visiting the UK. He does nonetheless represent one segment of the black community in America, and some support him as he expresses their resentment in an articulate manner. However, many more black Americans believe he is a violent extremist who propagates a message of racial hatred. Equally damaging are persistent accusations that the Nation of Islam has met with representatives of far-right racist groups such as the Ku Klux Klan, who would be strange bedfellows in the struggle for racial separatism. The Nation of Islam is certainly a problematic organisation to place in the civil rights movement, if indeed it can legitimately be linked to it. Its most famous disciple was Malcolm X, who left the movement and set up a splinter group.

Jackson and Farrakhan represent different aspects of the black struggle. The Nation of Islam supported Jackson's bid for the presidency in the 1980s, but should they be seen as part of the same movement? This is a difficult question to answer, and highlights how varied the differing strands of black action are. Such debates have been central to the struggle from the start, and coalesced in the 1950s and 1960s around the issue of non-violence and how to react to white oppression. As the civil rights movement progressed, the divisions between those who supported non-violence and those who became dissatis-fied with the gradualist approach became even more marked. After 1965 the movement also attracted criminal elements through organisations such as the Black Panthers. Some historians argue that after 1965 the black middle classes disengaged from the civil rights movement, which subsequently splintered and lost focus. Black leaders today such as Condoleezza Rice are not motivated by the civil rights rhetoric of decades ago. Some suggest that more radical groups such as the Nation of Islam have no clear agenda but plenty of racially motivated hatred and have hijacked the civil rights movement. Despite these divisions, race is still an important unifying factor politically. It is estimated that in Florida up to 90% of blacks voted for Obama in the 2008 election.

All white southerners were bad

Another common student mistake is automatically to equate the South with racism and the North with liberalism and equality. The real picture is more complex. There were liberal white southerners and racist white northerners. Blacks received support from progressive white southern authorities in many areas, but there was little credit for this. Arkansas, for example, had desegregated its public transport system in 1955 without controversy. It was only when the issue affected education that the Little Rock case (see Chapter 4) erupted. Many towns in the South desegregated their education system soon after *Brown* v *Board of Education of Topeka* with no fanfare, and life carried on as normal. Equally, there were states in other parts of the country where racism was as bad as anything in the Deep South. The state of Indiana, in the Midwest, was effectively run by the Ku Klux Klan in the mid-1920s. The governor and the members of the state Supreme Court were Klan-approved officials who abetted lynching and racist terrorism. Martin Luther King said that the worst racism he had ever experienced was in Chicago in 1967. In recent years some of the most serious racist incidents and tension have been in states outside the South. The Los Angeles riots of 1992 are just one example.

Any simple division between North and South ignores the complex picture of American politics in the period. The Democratic Coalition forged by Franklin Roosevelt in the 1930s rendered the idea of such a boundary invalid. Roosevelt joined the northern working class with southern 'Dixiecrats' to create a new national party capable of challenging the Republicans. The deal was that the northern liberals in the Democratic Party would not challenge the southern system and in return the southern Democrats would work with them to win the presidency. The Democratic Coalition was successful in getting the Democratic Party into the White House, but there was little chance of political change in the South as long as it remained intact.

Events in the 1950s and 1960s began to undermine the coalition, however. John F. Kennedy was elected in 1960 despite the fact that many southern Democrats hated him, and his initial unwillingness to intervene in civil rights issues can be explained by his reluctance to challenge the deal that brought him to power. But his successor, Lyndon Johnson, despite being a southerner, challenged the status quo by supporting civil rights. In response, Governor

George Wallace of Alabama split the Democratic Party, as southerners disgusted by Johnson's support for civil rights found a candidate they could vote for. At the same time Richard Nixon positioned himself to take advantage of the split, and in 1972 became the Republican candidate that disgruntled southerners could happily vote for.

The Democratic Coalition was formed to challenge the Republican stranglehold on the presidency. With the exception of Grover Cleveland and Woodrow Wilson, Republicans were in power between 1869 and 1933, becoming the 'natural ruling party' of America and enjoying a near monopoly of power. Roosevelt forged a coalition to challenge this, but it relied on the support of southern Democrats and so committed the party to maintaining segregation. Once Johnson 'broke the deal' in the 1960s, this coalition began to splinter. But he still enjoyed the support of some southern Democrats, as not all of them were opposed to reform. Today Republicans and Democrats are both represented in the South, and support for both parties is more complex and less geographic than it was in the 1950s and 1960s.

The civil rights movement ended in 1965

The passing of the Voting Rights Bill in 1965 meant that blacks could now vote: they had political power. This had been the final obvious hurdle in their quest for equality and the results were immediate. A generation of black politicians emerged in the South and took power. Before 1965 there were scarcely more than 100 black Americans in elected positions. By 1989 there were 7,200, and almost 5,000 of these were in the South. Prominent black politicians such as Barbara Jordan entered Congress in the 1970s. In the late 1980s Colin Powell, a black army general, became chairman of the joint chiefs of staff, the highest position in the US Army. He went on to become the first black secretary of state in 2001. Condoleezza Rice was appointed national security advisor in 2001 and secretary of state in 2005. Barrack Obama won the Democratic nomination in 2008 and was elected president in the same year.

Alongside these high profile political successes, affirmative action programmes were put in place that aimed at boosting black access to higher education and professional jobs. It seemed as if the discrimination of the past had finally been erased. However, there was still much left undone. Martin Luther King had switched his focus after 1965 to challenging economic inequality and had found that this was much harder to do. In August 1965 riots erupted in the Watts district of Los Angeles, leaving 34 dead. Other riots followed and black anger became more marked. The shift in the civil rights movement from the well-organised and peaceful campaigns of the 1950s and early 1960s to the more generalised and violent Black Power movement of the late 1960s and 1970s showed that times had changed. The assassination of Martin Luther King in 1968 was marked by widespread violence, and a palpable sense of disappointment began to overtake parts of the civil rights movement.

Richard Nixon, elected president in 1968, proved unwilling to enforce integration in the 1970s and the economic gap between whites and blacks continued to grow. In 1999 the Black Radical Congress stated that the 'struggle must continue, and with renewed vigour' until all Americans could 'enjoy full human rights, the fruits of their labour, and the freedom to realise their full human potential'. Inequality between the black and white communities has persisted, and many believe that blacks are still held back, albeit less obviously than in the South of the 1950s. Statistics vividly demonstrate this continuing inequality. In 2003 the US census showed that the median income for white households was $46,305, and $33,565 for Hispanics. Native Americas were on $32,116, while African-Americans were at the bottom of the ladder, with median incomes per household of $29,470. In 2007, according to a study by the University of Michigan, 24.5% of blacks and 21.5% of Hispanics were classified as poor, compared with just 8.2% of whites. Recent reports by the US Federal Reserve indicate that these gaps may be growing. In the South the differences are even more striking. In Mississippi, African-Americans make up 36% of the population but 75% of prisoners. The per capita income of blacks in Mississippi is 51% that of whites. In Alabama, 45% of blacks live below the poverty line. As Rev. Al Dixon stated: 'It's the same game with a different name. We now know that you can be free and broke. We can check into any hotel we want. But we can't pay the bill.'

Blacks in America face difficult choices. They also face new challenges. One of the developments that will define race relations in America in the twenty-first century is the growth of the Hispanic community. There are now more Hispanics than blacks in America, and by 2020, whites are likely to be in a minority in Texas, New Mexico, Arizona and Nevada. The Hispanic community has demanded to have the same rights and opportunities as their fellow Americans. They have also competed with the blacks for jobs and housing, arousing hostility and tension. In the South they have not had the same impact on the traditional racial fault lines, but in other regions the picture is more complicated. The Hispanic community argues that it faces discrimination too, and that it is also fighting for recognition of its civil rights.

Federal government played a minor role

Underestimation of the role played by the federal government is linked to a wider underestimation of the changing nature of the South in the 1950s and 1960s. We need to put the civil rights struggle in a wider context. After 1945 the South changed very quickly. To attract investment, southern states had to offer disciplined and cheap labour which was willing to be flexible in its working practices. Conflicts such as those that made Selma and Montgomery world-famous disrupted the economy and made the state governments involved look bad. It was clear that if states wanted to modernise and attract federal projects they would have to integrate, and in the 1960s most businesses started to do so. Houston in Texas became the centre of the space programme and gained billions of dollars in federal investment. Lyndon Johnson had made it clear that if the city wanted to get the programme it had to integrate. The National Aeronautics and Space Administration (NASA) was based in the South and could not be disrupted by civil rights agitation, so it had to be integrated from the start.

This economic pressure on southern states should not be underestimated. Integration made economic sense. The states that could offer stability would enjoy investment and succeed in modernising. It was the price of change — a price that southern states for the most part realised they would have to pay. Journalist Gary Younge highlights this point when he analyses the growth of the city of Atlanta since the segregated 1950s. He writes:

> Atlanta is the capital of what they call the New South, a place renowned for low wages and weak unions, which needed stability and well educated workers for capital to come flooding in. So long as segregation was maintained, this was never going to happen. But as racial barriers started coming down, the investors started rolling in. This was the South's reward for swapping racial bigotry for a place in the global economy, shedding its dependence on the rural and unskilled labour in favour of high-tech manufacturing and service industries.

It is a trade-off that has paid off, and blacks have even started returning to the South to look for employment in the new service sector. The US census has shown the black population in the South increasing year on year, as many former economic exiles who had escaped the poor prospects in the 1960s and 1970s realised that there were sometimes more opportunities in the desegregated South than in the supposedly integrated North.

In fact, over the last three decades the South as a whole has enjoyed impressive economic growth. Texas, Florida and Georgia all saw urban growth lead to the expansion of the automobile, telecommunications and textile industries. Technology, banking and aviation firms have also located their businesses in the former Confederate states. By 2000 some of the southern states were growing faster than any in the North, and many well-known businesses were based in the region. Dallas, Houston, Atlanta, Miami, Austin and Charlotte have all grown into major cities. The service economy has boomed, and tourism has also become a key employer in Florida and the Gulf coast. Major firms setting up new plants in the South include Mercedes-Benz in Tuscaloosa and Hyundai in Montgomery, both in Alabama. BMW has opened a new production facility in Spartanburg, South Carolina and General Motors has one in Spring Hill, Tennessee. Nissan's North American headquarters are located in Franklin, also in Tennessee. Huntsville, Alabama, is home to the Cummings Research Park (the fourth largest in the world), while major banking corporations such as the Bank of America, SunTrust and Compass have also located their operations in the South. Images of the 'Old South' and cotton-picking or tobacco plantations are increasingly out of date. The South today is high tech, urban and expanding. Parts of the South have some of the lowest unemployment rates in the USA.

Questions

1 Why are standard views of the civil rights movement sometimes wrong?
2 Is it fair to regard the civil rights movement as mainly concerning African-Americans?
3 'Economic changes in the South were as effective as protest in ending segregation.' Discuss whether you agree with this viewpoint.

How did the segregated system in the South develop?

To understand the civil rights movement of the 1950s it is necessary to understand the way that America developed. The civil rights movement must be seen in the context of slavery and the failure to reconstruct the South after the Civil War.

Slavery

When North America was colonised, the use of slaves became widespread in some states. This was linked to the slave trade in the Caribbean, where the sugar plantations relied on slave labour. A triangular pattern of trade developed: ships took slaves from Africa to the Caribbean and North America, from where they transported rum and tobacco to England, where the captains took on money as well as cloth, iron and other products to exchange for more slaves.

The evils of the slave trade are well known; many Africans died on the 'middle passage' to the New World or soon after arrival. North America counted for only a small proportion of the slaves trafficked: South America and the sugar islands absorbed far more. About 400,000 Africans (5% of the total) found themselves transported to slavery in the British colonies of North America. Once in North America, they were normally sold in the 'southern' states of Maryland, Virginia, the Carolinas and Georgia. These states were based on plantation-style farming and needed large numbers of labourers for their most successful crops: first tobacco and then cotton. There were slaves in the 'northern' states, such as New Jersey, but they were fewer in number and as these states developed they had less need of slaves.

Slavery created a system that was not only deeply unfair and inhumane but also very obviously against the spirit of the Constitution. It became more widespread as time passed. The invention of the cotton gin in 1793, which speeded up the processing of raw cotton, meant that slavery became even more vital to the southern states in which it was practised.

At the same time, there was growing sentiment against slavery in the North and across the world. Britain's Slavery Abolition Act of 1833 made slavery illegal in the British Empire. Further action followed, with the British government declaring that the slave trade was piracy and intervening to stop it by seizing slave ships and freeing the slaves. It also took action against slave-dealing in Africa and signed anti-slavery treaties with African rulers. The international slave trade was largely ended by such actions, but within America it continued. The slave states had such large native African-American populations that they did not need to import any more slaves and simply traded internally. However, the international condemnation of slavery helped American abolitionists win increasing audiences for their message, and from the 1830s the abolition of slavery became an issue in American political life.

The Civil War

The Civil War pushed the issue of slavery to the forefront of American politics. Abolition was not an initial war aim but in 1863 it became one. The Emancipation Proclamation of 22 September 1862 declared that if any state was still in rebellion by New Year's Day 1863, the slaves in that state would be 'forever free'. The deadline was ignored by the southern states and so abolition became an inevitable consequence of victory. The importance of the Emancipation Proclamation is clear. It promised to bring freedom to former slaves. The defeat of the Confederate states on 9 April 1865 was total and offered the opportunity for a complete reconstruction of the South.

Slavery was abolished, but other reforms could also have been implemented. The freed slaves would need access to education and the right to vote. They would need support in terms of land and livestock so that they could support themselves (they were promised '40 acres and a mule'). They would also need equal access to justice, and rights to the same legal process as whites. If significant progress towards equality was going to be made, the abolition of slavery was really just the start. Unfortunately for many it was the end: although slavery was abolished, the power structure in the South was barely altered, and within two decades of the end of the war the blacks were in almost as bad a position as they had been before it started. Why was this historic opportunity squandered? Why would it take another century for blacks in the South to achieve rights that were guaranteed in the Constitution and that were hard fought for in the Civil War?

Inequality after the Civil War

Many in the North were aware of the importance of making sure that reforms and effective reconstruction followed the defeat of the South. The initial terms of the victory were lenient. Confederate forces were disbanded and promised freedom provided they did not continue to fight. Lincoln recognised that there was enough bitterness in the South without additional punitive measures. However, he was serious about sorting out the issues surrounding slavery. Unfortunately he would never get the chance to demonstrate this: on 14 April 1865 he was shot by an assassin and he died the next day. The new president was Andrew Johnson, a southerner from Tennessee. He was ill-suited to the difficulties of dealing with the southern states.

The Thirteenth Amendment to the US Constitution passed on 6 December 1865 ended slavery, but Johnson followed it with a number of actions that seemed to support the South. He failed to stop the southern states initiating a series of laws in 1865–66 that became known as the Black Codes and that limited the rights of former slaves. They could not own guns, testify against a white man in court, vote, or serve on juries. They were forbidden to marry or have sexual relations with whites and they were excluded from many jobs. Segregation on transport was swiftly enforced. Blacks were also subject to strict vagrancy laws that allowed them to be hired out to planters or other employers if they failed to show a work contract.

This racist attitude may seem baffling to us today. Why did so many southern whites hate the blacks so much? Why could they not accept them as equals? Why, when they had lost the Civil War, could they not have allowed them their freedom and the chance to fulfil their potential? The answer is complex and difficult to explain. The slavery system had been a historic fact for generations and many whites felt it was part of the natural order. Many white slave-owners found it difficult to accept how much the slaves had hated their servitude. Many of them felt betrayed by the desertion of the blacks to the Unionist cause during the war. They were also bitter at their defeat, and the blacks were an obvious scapegoat. They seemed determined to oppress the blacks beyond the point of rational explanation. The wave of violence against blacks that accompanied the introduction of the Black Codes was a case in point.

The failure of reconstruction

The Ku Klux Klan was founded on Christmas Eve 1865. Initially its main aim was to scare the freedmen and those perceived as helping them. However, the

Klan quickly became still more sinister and began extending its activities to arson and murder. Race riots broke out in various southern cities, showing the extent of hatred felt towards the freed slaves. In Memphis in April 1866, riots left 46 blacks dead. In New Orleans on 30 July worse followed: 40 people, mainly blacks, were killed and many more injured by the police force under orders from the mayor. Blacks accused of various crimes were summarily executed by armed mobs: racially motivated violence had become part of the way of life in the South.

It was clear to many in the North that the end of the Civil War had not achieved the promised freedoms that the slaves had yearned for. Congress tried to support African-Americans in the South, and there were some impressive strides towards equality during this period of 'Congressional reconstruction', but it soon began to lose its focus on the issue. White supremacists also began to organise more effectively against the measures introduced, and over time the tide began to turn against the reformers and back in favour of the racists. The Democratic Party enjoyed a revival of fortunes and began to take control of most of the southern states, until the Republicans controlled only four. These states too soon fell to the Democrats. The growing power of the Democrats and divisions in the Republican Party signalled the end of reconstruction in the South. By 1877 the freed slaves and their northern allies had been defeated in their attempts to achieve equality. Southern racist attitudes and entrenched interests in perpetuating the system of inequality had endured and outlasted attempts to reform them. The cause of civil rights would now be put back so far that it would take another 100 years to get back to the situation that had been achieved by 1869.

Jim Crow

The magnitude of this defeat was soon apparent to blacks. The failure of reconstruction left them at the mercy of the newly revived Democratic Party and an openly racist political establishment determined to ensure they remained second-class citizens. Essentially they were abandoned by the Republican Party, which, as Adam Fairclough wrote, had 'wearied of a policy that had become a political albatross'. He continues: 'The violence that accompanied elections in the former Confederacy no longer aroused public opinion…Shrewdly calculating that it could still capture the White House with northern votes alone, the Republican Party allowed the Democrats to "redeem" the South.' The consequences of this decision would be disastrous for the 4 million blacks living in the South as they saw the few precious gains in liberty after Emancipation quickly swept away.

The first step was to deny the blacks the vote. Once this was achieved, more oppression could follow. Blacks were effectively shut out of the political process. In the wake of this, further exclusions followed: education, transport and public services were segregated and a system of 'apartheid' was effectively instituted.

The increase in lynchings of blacks accused of various crimes was testimony to this. Black men accused of rape or sexual misconduct with white women were most likely to end up as victims of lynch mobs. A common image peddled by white racists at the time was that of predatory and violent black men attacking the virginal and virtuous white woman. An accusation was enough to see them hanged or beaten to death by enraged white mobs. W. Fitzhugh Brundage estimates that between 1880 and 1930 southern lynch mobs executed 3,320 blacks (723 whites were also killed in this way). The South accounted for 95% of the national total of lynchings by 1930 and blacks represented 91% of that total. Lynching was clearly an exercise in power rather than justice. The fact that white mobs could murder blacks without a trial and without suffering any consequences themselves was a brutal demonstration of race relations in the South. Lynching scared the black population of the South into submission. The issue of lynching became one of the first causes around which a new civil rights movement began to form. One of the first effective civil rights campaigns in America in the late nineteenth and early twentieth centuries was that led by a young black woman from Memphis, Tennessee, Ida B. Wells, to outlaw lynching.

The southern states gradually erected a comprehensive system aimed at denying blacks civil rights, which became known as the 'Jim Crow' laws. These laws regulated all aspects of life for blacks and denied them any chance of equality. Literacy tests prevented them from voting, separate schools ensured they were educationally worse off than whites, and they were also forced to eat and travel in segregated restaurants and transport. The efforts of the whites to prevent southern blacks from achieving full civil rights were supported by the Supreme Court (later, ironically, the institution that would be responsible for overturning many of the same laws). In 1876 the Supreme Court ruled in *United States* v *Reese* that Kentucky electoral officials who had turned away black voters were allowed to do this and ruled that the Fifteenth Amendment did not automatically give people the right to vote — it was the states that could decide this. In 1876 in the *United States* v *Cruikshank* decision nine Ku Klux Klan members had their indictments overturned: they argued that a federal court could not try them after they had attacked a political meeting of blacks, killing or wounding more than 100 of them. In 1883 sections of the 1875 Civil Rights Act were ruled unconstitutional, and segregation in private enterprises was allowed.

The biggest blow to civil rights campaigners came in the Supreme Court decision of *Plessy* v *Ferguson* in May 1896. The Supreme Court ruled that the segregation of railway carriages in Louisiana was justified on the principle of 'separate but equal'. This was a body blow to black attempts to challenge the growing racism of southern society. The ruling also extended this 'separate but equal' principle to schools, although it was obvious that the southern states had no intention of providing equal funding for black and white schools (in 1900, for example, they spent $4.91 per white student and $2.21 per black student per annum). Overall, life for blacks in the South was harsh. They lived in poor housing, were badly educated and were kept tied to menial farm work by a sharecropping system that allowed them to 'rent' land and farm it for a 'share' of the profits that rarely materialised.

Blacks in the South

How, then, were blacks to respond to this treatment? First, it should be noted that their options were limited. The speed with which the southern state governments had rolled back the freedoms won between 1861 and 1875 took many by surprise. Second, it must be remembered that their isolation was also a factor — the North seemed uninterested and in fact even hostile to blacks. In addition to this they were not allowed to vote and were denied any opportunity to alter the system politically and peacefully. Rebellion was virtually impossible, as the entire police and judicial system was constructed to deny them any chance of successful protest and the lynch mob was ready to make that very obvious. Finally, there was little chance of mobilising international intervention in the early 1900s. Essentially they were on their own.

In this context blacks in the South in 1900 had two real choices. The first was to move north: the expansion of industry was creating opportunities, and although blacks were excluded from many jobs there were some chances to better themselves. The second option was to accommodate themselves to the state of things as they were in the South and try to get on with it. At this stage the potential third course of action — to protest and to attempt to achieve reform — was not really an option: conditions in the South were too oppressive to allow any change and the black community at this stage did not have the organisation or leadership to initiate it. Protest would come, but not yet. In fact, the first attempts to initiate reform would come from blacks in the North allying with white liberals to try to get change onto the agenda. The only exception to this was Ida B. Wells' anti-lynching campaign, which was based in the South and supported by the National Association of Colored Women (NACW). However, opposition soon forced Ida to leave Memphis and take her campaign to national and international audiences. As it was also really a single-issue campaign, there were differences between this and later protests.

Many blacks took the first option and voted with their feet. They left the South to seek new lives elsewhere. Some argued they should return to Africa (an idea that would become popular again in the 1920s and later in the 1950s and 1960s). Others argued they should create new communities in America. In the 1870s and 1880s there had been a short-lived campaign to settle in Kansas and over 80,000 blacks had moved there to start farmsteads. These 'Exodusters' (after the Bible book of Exodus, with its story of the Jews leaving captivity in Egypt for the Promised Land) rapidly ran into familiar problems, as racism and fear of being 'swamped' by black settlers meant that whites soon pushed to stop them. The project failed and many returned south. Other all-black communities were formed in various states, but these schemes had a number of drawbacks and were not attractive to many blacks. The only real place to start again was in the industrial North, but this was a real challenge. Many southern blacks lacked the skills and money to move and had few friends and relations to help them settle there. There was also widespread discrimination, which meant jobs were hard to get. Between 1890 and 1910 about 200,000 blacks escaped the South for the North — a small proportion of the total population of 10 million.

The rest had to put up with their situation. They might have disliked the system in the South and wanted change but they had lives to lead. Some even made a virtue of necessity and argued that this was the best option. They would work within the system and prove to the whites that they were worthy of being accepted as equals. This policy of accommodation found its most articulate and successful spokesman in Booker T. Washington. A former slave who became the most respected black leader of his age, Washington was much criticised at the time (and after his death) for his willingness to compromise with the white supremacist system in the South. However, given the limitations of the age and the system in which he was operating, modern commentators are more sympathetic and willing to concede that he achieved significant success in furthering some aspects of the southern blacks' cause.

Booker T. Washington tried to give blacks the means to make accommodation with the system and still maintain their dignity. He became the most influential black spokesman of his generation after setting up the first all-black educational establishment, the Tuskegee Institute. This was founded in 1881 and focused on teaching vocational trades such as carpentry, farming and mechanical engineering to blacks. Washington believed that blacks would gain their political and social freedoms after proving themselves capable of economic ability. By 1894 the Tuskegee Institute had 54 officers and teachers and was educating hundreds of black students. Growing publicity generated more funds and Washington became an increasingly influential man.

Some argued that Washington's gradualist approach was not enough. They wanted more, and soon he was being criticised by other black leaders, particularly those from the North who looked at conditions in the South and felt that change should come. One of his most vocal critics was W. E. B. Du Bois. Du Bois was an academic who had studied in Berlin and also at Harvard University — he was the first African-American to receive a doctorate. He was a professor of economics and history at Atlanta University from 1896 to 1910 and had been critical of Washington's attempts to compromise with the white establishment in the South from the beginning. In 1903 he wrote an essay, 'Of Mr Booker T. Washington and others', which was published in his book, *The Souls of Black Folk*. He argued:

> Mr Washington represents in Negro thought the old attitude of adjustment and submission…Mr Washington distinctly argues that black people give up, at least for the present, three things. First, political power. Second, insistence on civil rights. Third, higher education of Negro youth.

Du Bois believed that this was going too far and would not allow blacks to make 'effective progress'. More needed to be done: political reform must be fought for.

First civil rights campaigners

In July 1905 a group of blacks met on the Canadian side of the Niagara Falls to decide how best to proceed with a plan of action. There were 29 of them, mostly well educated and successful. The Niagara Movement wanted 'organised, determined and aggressive action on the part of men who believe in Negro freedom and growth'. The principal spokesmen of the group were Du Bois and William Monroe Trotter. Their proposals and the language they adopted marked a clear split from the policy of accommodation advocated by Booker T. Washington. Instead of accepting the system in the South they would challenge it, and they would also work for full equality in the North.

The Niagara Movement marked a decisive new phase in the struggle for civil rights. Educated and determined black community leaders were set on trying to bring about political reform. They were also hostile to Washington and those who wanted to compromise with the system. Relations between Du Bois and Washington soon descended into a state of open hatred. Washington could not accept his critics, and the 'Wizard of Tuskegee' was fierce in his condemnation of any challengers to his position as pre-eminent leader of the black community in America. He dismissed his northern critics as agitators — intellectuals with little understanding of life for the blacks in the South.

In response his critics argued that he was blocking progress for blacks, monopolising the debate and cooperating with the white political establishment in suppressing dissent. Each side failed to see the good in the other. Washington did try to support blacks, and in his role as advisor to President Theodore Roosevelt he tried to mitigate racist policies. Du Bois and others were also well intentioned, seeing that more was needed than simply working hard and hoping that the whites would give them some freedoms sometime. The two approaches could have been complementary, but unfortunately hostility prevented this. The division within the black community continued throughout the civil rights movement.

As in many other movements there were moderates and radicals as well as gradualists and people who wanted rapid results. Later there would be those who advocated peaceful protest while others wanted violence. There were also separatists who believed that blacks would never get fair treatment from the whites and that they should emigrate to Africa or set up separate communities in America. With a number of volatile personalities and the normal squabbles for power that affect any organisation, the black movement was as marked by dissent and division as any other.

The Niagara Movement met again in 1906 at Harpers Ferry, West Virginia, determined to effect change. The need for change was underlined by continuing racial violence and oppression. Riots in Springfield, Illinois, in August 1908 saw two blacks lynched, six shot dead and over 2,000 forced to flee the city. There was no federal response. This contrasted strongly with President Theodore Roosevelt's response in August 1906, when two white men died in a bar brawl with a number of black soldiers from the 25th Infantry Regiment (the Indian-fighting 'Buffalo soldiers'). The army failed to prove the guilt of a single man or even to substantiate what had happened, but he nevertheless disbanded three entire companies of the regiment (176 men) without pension rights.

It had also become clear to white liberals that the blacks were labouring against impossible odds to achieve equality. Some believed that they should become involved in the civil rights movement and offered to join up with the leaders of the Niagara Movement. At the National Conference on the Negro in May 1909, white and black community leaders agreed that the 'systematic persecution of law-abiding citizens and their disenfranchisement on account of their race alone is a crime'. With this statement the NAACP was born: it would become the most influential organisation fighting for equal rights for blacks for a generation, and many of the victories the movement enjoyed in the 1950s and 1960s would be due, at least in part, to its actions.

The NAACP needed to prove its worth and mounted a series of legal challenges to segregation that met with mixed results. It won an injunction against a theatre in New York that refused to seat blacks, and managed to challenge voting restrictions in Oklahoma. However, the South remained resolutely segregated and the federal government as uninterested in black rights as ever. The NAACP grew slowly in the period. By 1916 it had 8,785 members, with 68 branches in the North and three in the South. But there was little prospect of it achieving significant success without some corresponding social changes. The black community in America was still too powerless to achieve real improvements. It needed increased wealth and opportunity, and recognition from the white community that change was required. As it turned out, the next 30 years would be the most momentous in American history.

Questions

1 'Reconstruction failed in the South because the Republicans abandoned the region to the Democrats.' Discuss this viewpoint on the failure of reconstruction.
2 'Blacks in the South had little alternative to "accommodation" in this period.' How far do you agree with this view?
3 Why did white liberals from the North dominate the early civil rights movement?

Why did the world wars fail to result in freedom for blacks?

The First World War (1914–1918) and the Second World War (1939–45) would transform the prospects of the civil rights movement in a number of ways. The First World War allowed many to move north and advance themselves economically. Many others were conscripted and proved themselves in service to their country. The postwar period, however, saw any temporary concessions rapidly reversed. The Second World War had a more far-reaching impact. The defeat of Nazi Germany and Japan discredited political systems based on theories of racial superiority and undermined white supremacists' arguments to justify segregation. The demands of the wartime economy allowed blacks to compete with whites in hitherto closed industries. As in the First World War, conscription of blacks into segregated regiments was the norm, but they proved they could fight as well as whites when given the chance. Segregation in the armed forces ended in 1948, and during the Korean War (1950–53) units were mixed, with blacks treated the same as whites. On their return from conflict in Europe and Asia, black soldiers asked pertinent questions about the lack of political freedoms in their own country and were influential in instilling a new confidence and militancy in the civil rights struggle.

The First World War

The First World War allowed many blacks a chance to escape their subsistence-level existence in the South. About 330,000 blacks moved to the North between 1915 and 1918 and were quick to take advantage of new opportunities. The American economy geared up to supply the fighting nations with supplies and a boom ensued. At the same time emigration from Europe was halted and a labour shortage resulted. Railroad construction, steel mills, automobile plants and packing houses all needed labour. Industries that had kept blacks out now welcomed them. In Detroit the car manufacturers Packard and Ford hired black men, while black women found jobs in kitchens and laundries. Some factories began hiring agents to go south and recruit blacks and pay their fares to resettle. When the USA entered the war, blacks were conscripted into the forces. Between 1917 and 1918 200,000 blacks were drafted and 42,000 saw combat. A segregated officer training school was set up at Fort des Moines, Iowa, in 1917.

But the opportunities offered to blacks did not last. At the end of the war many whites showed resentment towards returning veterans. Race riots in 1919–20 targeted discharged servicemen and disillusionment was swift. Blacks returning to the South found that little had changed; in fact hostility had increased. Southern whites, worried that black ex-servicemen might apply their newly acquired military skills to their old resentments, were quick to put them in their place and in some cases were almost hysterical in their fear of blacks. The fact that many in the black community were advocating more militancy seemed to confirm their fears. Du Bois had stated in May 1919, 'We return fighting.' Having fought for democracy in Europe, he wrote, 'we are cowards and jackasses if…we do not marshal every ounce of our brain and brawn to fight a sterner, longer, more unbending battle against the forces of hell in our own land'. A newspaper set up by two young blacks, Chandler Owen and A. Philip Randolph, called on blacks to organise and revolt. *The Messenger* welcomed the Bolshevik Revolution in Russia. This new confidence was apparent to those in power. Emmett J. Scott, Special Adjutant to the Secretary of War, Newton D. Baker, commented in 1919: 'Intelligent Negroes…who got some idea of the real liberty in France, although they were not permitted to enjoy it overmuch, are united in demanding better treatment from the American people.'

The interwar period

There was little chance of the black population getting the better treatment it demanded. White America was not keen to give the blacks anything, and riots in the North and South confirmed this. More than 40 blacks were killed during riots marked by terrible violence in Illinois in July 1917, which showed that racism was not just a southern problem. A few weeks later black soldiers from the 24th US Infantry Regiment stationed in Camp Logan in Texas went on the rampage after suffering months of 'Jim Crow' rules, killing five policemen and 12 other whites. Clearly race relations were not improving. In addition to the wave of postwar riots and killings, the Ku Klux Klan was reorganised and revived and broader in its scope than before. It organised against black communities and also against Jews, Catholics and any other group that it deemed 'un-American'. Its new leader was William J. Simmons (a former minister of the Methodist Episcopal Church), who managed to expand it into the North and Midwest, so that by 1921 it claimed more than 100,000 members. In 1922 the Klan was taken over by Hiram Wesley Evans, who took the organisation to new strength. By 1924 it had over 4 million members.

It was in this atmosphere of racial hatred and frustration that a new voice advocating an old solution to black problems was heard. Marcus Garvey, a Jamaican, had arrived in America in 1916 to raise funds for a Jamaican version of Booker T. Washington's Tuskegee Institute. He was the founder and president of the Universal Negro Improvement Association (UNIA) and advocated a number of positions, some familiar and some new. Some of these would reappear in the 1950s and 1960s, forming a potent mixture of ideas that appealed to many blacks. Marcus Garvey wanted blacks in America to realise the international dimension of their problems. He urged them to look to Africa and to link their struggle with that of the Africans seeking to free themselves from imperial rule. Du Bois had also realised that the end of the First World War should result in freedom for African colonies and argued: 'This war ought to result in the establishment of an independent Negro central African republic.' Garvey was more militant than this, declaring that 'Africa must be for the Africans' and that blacks should be prepared to fight for independence.

The UNIA grew in 1919–20 into a major national organisation and Marcus Garvey filled a power vacuum in black leadership left by the death of Booker T. Washington in 1915. At the height of its influence it had far more members than the NAACP. (How many was unclear, as Garvey exaggerated its numbers: he claimed up to 6 million members, but in fact the total was nearer 100,000.) It also offered black Americans new hope. First, he cleverly linked their fate to that of Africa and convinced them that as a people they had both an important historic past and also a great future. They were part of a Negro race that numbered hundreds of millions and so had massive potential power. Second, he offered them a solution — emigration. The UNIA would be a government-in-waiting, ready to take control of Africa when liberation occurred. He stated: 'The Negro must have a country, and a nation of his own. If you laugh at this idea then you are selfish and wicked.'

Garvey set up various businesses to support his enterprise, the most notable being the Black Star Line, an international black steamship company in which he sold hundreds of thousands of shares. He also presided over the First International Convention of Negro Peoples of the World in 1920, with delegates from 24 countries. Once Africa was liberated, he argued, American blacks should migrate there to find equality. Marcus Garvey's 'Back to Africa' project appealed to many in America and from 1920 to 1924 his popularity grew.

However, the idea of separate countries or destinies for blacks and whites could only ever have limited practicability. As with the Exodusters in the 1870s and the Nation of Islam after the 1960s, such a philosophy would only appeal to the most radical and dissatisfied. Most blacks argued that they should not have to leave their homeland to receive equal treatment and that they did not want to be separated from the whites. Moreover, such schemes played into the hands of white supremacists and essentially granted the racists victory. This was demonstrated in June 1922, when Garvey met with Ku Klux Klan leader Edward Young Clarke to discuss expanding the UNIA's activities into the South. This action convinced many in the black community that Garvey was at best deluded, and at worst criminal. The NAACP ran a 'Garvey must go' campaign and many concluded that he did not represent real opportunities for black Americans. In 1925 he faced fraud charges as the Black Star Line collapsed and he was sentenced to serve 5 years in prison. He was released early, and deported in 1927. His influence rapidly waned and he died in London in 1940.

The interwar period saw another potential avenue in the black civil rights struggle open and then, as with Garveyism, close. The Bolshevik Revolution of 1917 had turned Russia into the Union of Soviet Socialist Republics (the USSR) and inspired a whole new generation of radicals across the world to work for a new age of social justice through communism. The fact that the socialist dream would turn into a totalitarian nightmare was not yet apparent, and the 1920s and 1930s saw many intelligent and idealistic young people support communism. In America the Communist movement was overtly non-racist and offered blacks full equality in the struggle to bring about the revolution. The Communist Party of the USA (CPUSA) enjoyed its greatest influence in this period, and through its involvement in the Scottsboro case showed that radical left-wing agitators could be as effective as the NAACP or any other organisation in challenging racism.

The Scottsboro Affair of 1931 was an example of a single criminal case becoming a flashpoint illuminating greater injustices. Like the trial of O. J. Simpson in 1995, or that of the police officers who attacked Rodney King 3 years earlier, this case was largely about race. A scuffle between black and white boys trying to hitch a ride in a railway freight car (a common way of travelling about America in the Depression years) developed into a rape trial. Police pulled nine black youths, between 12 and 20 years old, off a freight wagon after fighting had broken out with some white boys trying to climb into the same wagon. Two white girls also pulled off the wagon at the same time alleged that they had been repeatedly raped by the black youths. Why the girls said they had been raped has never become clear. Traditionally such a charge would have resulted in a rapid lynching, and it was perhaps testimony to the changing times (and perhaps the effect of Ida B. Wells' campaign) that the governor of Alabama despatched troops to protect the suspects. In the ensuing trial, eight of the accused were found guilty of rape and sentenced to death.

The case against one of them, Roy Wright, was declared a mistrial. The trial had been concluded in 4 days and relied wholly on the testimony of the two white girls, Ruby Bates and Victoria Price. Doctors examining the girls had found no evidence of a struggle, although it was clear that they had engaged in sexual activity at some stage in the preceding days, probably before boarding the train. The attitude of the locals was best summed up by local Birmingham congressman George Huddleston, who stated:

> I don't care whether they are innocent or guilty. They were found riding on the same freight car with two white women and that's enough for me. It doesn't matter what the women had done previously. I'm in favour of the boys being executed just as quickly as possible. You can't understand how we southern gentlemen feel about this question of relationships between Negro men and white women.

The injustice of the trial was apparent to any neutral observer, yet the NAACP was reluctant to get involved. Instead the Communist Party stepped in. The Scottsboro case quickly became a cause célèbre and attracted widespread interest. After a number of trials and varying sentences the Scottsboro defendants served jail terms but were out by 1950. The Communist Party had saved the boys from certain death, although the involvement of the NAACP later in the case also helped get the accused freed.

The Scottsboro case was the most high-profile intervention by the Communist Party in race relations, but the party campaigned for racial equality throughout this period. It was also happy to promote blacks to positions of leadership in the party, and some of its key players in the 1950s started out in the party in the 1930s. However, despite some successes, the Communists were unlikely to change life for the majority of the blacks. They were held in too much suspicion by the government and by the overwhelming majority of Americans, black as well as white.

As the 1930s drew to a close, the civil rights struggle for blacks was still very much caught in stasis. Black people had achieved some increased wealth and opportunity in the North. Marcus Garvey's Black Nationalism and the Communist Party's brotherhood of the proletariat had both offered some hope of a future beyond racial oppression, but both had offered false promise. The NAACP was still chipping away at the complex edifice of racial oppression without major success, and in the South the situation was much the same as before the war. Jim Crow laws regulated all areas of black life, and while lynchings might have subsided and some blacks had prospered they were still denied the vote, decent schooling and access to employment in the professions. Another period of change would be needed to allow increased fluidity and a chance to redraw race relations. The Second World War would usher in that period of change.

The Second World War

In the Second World War black Americans faced the same dangers of military service as their white counterparts, but for the civilian black community it brought new opportunities. The recession of the 1930s was soon a distant memory as the wartime economy boomed. The armaments industries sucked in labour and offered blacks new jobs. Welders, skilled craftsmen and labourers were all in demand and blacks were once again quick to sense an opportunity. They were also more politically astute than in 1914 and better organised. Labour disputes in the 1930s had developed their negotiating skills. A strike by the Brotherhood of Sleeping Car Porters (BSCP), which was entirely black, had resulted in better pay. Its leader, Philip Randolph (joint founder of the left-wing newspaper *The Messenger*), was also the president of the National Negro Congress (formed in 1936 in Chicago), and his March on Washington Movement (MOWM) united disparate black groups behind it.

Randolph realised that wartime conditions had put black workers in a position of advantage. In January 1941 he declared that the 'whole national defence set-up reeks and stinks of race prejudice, hatred and discrimination' and threatened a mass march on the White House by the black community if President Franklin Roosevelt did not promise equal opportunities to blacks in the wartime industries. He excluded whites from the march in order to minimise Communist influence and to maximise black pride. In the face of this Roosevelt bowed to pressure and issued Executive Order 8802 on 25 June 1941, prohibiting racial discrimination in the defence industry and setting up a Committee on Fair Employment Practice to supervise and support the directive.

Black participation in wartime industries increased from 3% to 9%, and approximately 2 million blacks were employed in industry. Black membership of unions rose to 1,250,000, while a further 3 million blacks were registered for military service. In 1944 the armed forces included almost 900,000 blacks. Many saw combat and, as in the First World War, significant numbers of black officers were trained to lead their units. They also fought well. In the 1944 Battle of the Bulge, black soldiers mixed with white soldiers. As Captain Wesley J. Simons of Snow Hill stated: 'They fit into our company like any other platoon, and they fight like hell.'

As well as being more organised, blacks were aware that they had to use the opportunity offered by the war to bring about change. The First World War had promised much but delivered little. This time would be different. The fight for freedom abroad would be matched by progress at home. The Pittsburgh newspaper, *The Courier*, started the 'Double V' campaign: for victory abroad against fascism and at home against racism and segregation. The NAACP saw its membership expand from 50,000 to over 450,000. For the first time it was truly a mass member organisation. In 1942 another important organisation was founded: the Congress of Racial Equality (CORE). Initially small in numbers, it advocated non-violent direct action to challenge segregation. Inspired by Gandhi in India, its leaders Bayard Rustin, Bernice Fisher and James Farmer would all become heavily involved in the postwar struggle for civil rights in the South.

However, despite this sense that new changes were on the horizon, little had actually altered where it mattered most, in the South. In 1947 CORE co-sponsored the Journey of Reconciliation with a British-based pacifist organisation, the Fellowship of Reconciliation. They only confronted segregation in the upper South (states such as Virginia and North Carolina) but were still arrested on several occasions and two of them were sentenced to 30 days' hard labour in North Carolina. A third and fourth, both white, were sentenced to 90 days' hard labour. The judge made his reasons clear, telling Igal Roodenko and Joseph Felmet:

> It's about time you Jews from New York learned that you can't come down here bringing your niggers with you to upset the customs of the South. Just to teach you a lesson, I gave your black boys 30 days, and I give you 90.

Freedom denied

By the time the Second World War ended in 1945 it had advanced the cause of civil rights in a number of ways. First, the NAACP had become a mass movement, and was now half a million strong. Second, Roosevelt had been forced to act against discrimination in the defence industry, so millions more blacks had been able to take jobs from which they had previously been excluded. Third, blacks had once again proved they were capable soldiers if they were allowed to fight. Fourth, the fight against fascism had highlighted the obvious iniquities of the segregation system in the South — how could America be the 'land of the free' when so many were denied basic rights guaranteed them by the Constitution?

The new president in office at the end of the war, Harry S. Truman, who succeeded Roosevelt in April 1945, was more sympathetic to black grievances. He established a Committee on Civil Rights in 1946 after a black ex-serviceman called George Dorsey was murdered along with his wife and two friends in a wave of racial violence that marked the end of the war and once again focused on returning soldiers. On 29 October 1947 this committee released a report, *To Secure These Rights*. The report argued that civil rights abuses should be redressed for three reasons: moral, economic and international. It made more than 35 recommendations for action, including an anti-lynching law and a fair employment practices commission, along with an end to segregation on public transport. On 28 August 1948 Truman issued Executive Order 9981, ending segregation in the armed forces, and publicly stated his commitment to civil rights.

Questions

1 Why did the First World War not result in greater civil rights for the blacks?

2 Why did Marcus Garvey's UNIA fail?

3 Why was the Second World War so important in changing the fortunes of the civil rights movement?

How did blacks challenge segregation after 1945?

Despite the developments in the years up to and including the Second World War, in the southern states conditions for blacks had hardly improved since the failure of reconstruction in the 1870s. In the 1930s the NAACP had sent Charles Houston, the vice-dean of Howard University School of Law, to document educational facilities in the South and what he had seen was depressing. In South Carolina the state spent ten times as much on educating white children as it did on educating black children. Florida, Mississippi, Alabama and Georgia spent five times more money on white children than on black. At this stage 9 million blacks lived in the South, and this educational deprivation was just one of many obstacles they faced. Charles Houston had built up an effective law school for blacks after teaching at Howard University, the largest all-black college in the USA. He realised that if blacks wanted to challenge the racism they faced, one of the most effective ways to do so would be to challenge it in court — legally. He also realised that black lawyers wanting to challenge segregation would have to be well versed in constitutional law. The Fourteenth and Fifteenth Amendments guaranteed the blacks equal rights. The southern states' and Supreme Court decisions in the 1880s and 1890s had denied them what was rightfully theirs.

The NAACP and the South

The NAACP was initially mainly based in the North but it slowly built up a presence in the South. Charles Houston was in charge of planning an effective strategy. He decided that the way to challenge the complex and entrenched system of segregation in the South was to approach the problem in a long-term and gradual way. First, the NAACP would challenge segregation in the higher educational establishments such as graduate schools. Then it would work its way downwards, through colleges, high schools and elementary schools. He decided to focus on graduate schools, because so few blacks went to them that most states did not provide separate ones. He could challenge them more easily here, as the Plessy defence of 'separate but equal' was hard to argue when states provided no facilities for blacks to study in a particular area, such as law. Houston also argued that desegregating education should be the NAACP's primary goal, on the grounds that educational segregation was the most important factor crippling blacks' prospects in the South.

The other obvious issue on which blacks needed to mount an effective challenge to the system of segregation was voting rights. Without the ability to vote, blacks had little chance of changing the system, and could effectively be ignored. Changing the complex system by which the southern states had stopped blacks voting would be hard work. Voter registration campaigns and challenges to various 'literacy' tests to which blacks where subjected, which were unfair and deliberately aimed at excluding them, were the two main ways in which the NAACP tried to address this. There was also the challenge of ending segregation on transport, in public places and in restaurants. Finally (and most problematic) was the high level of institutional and generalised violence against blacks. Lynching might be less common, but it was still clear to blacks that if they stepped out of line they would face harsh retribution. The police and various 'citizen' groups would prove to be violent and committed adversaries throughout the civil rights years, and many blacks and whites working for change would face violence.

This threat of violence meant that change in the South came slowly, and many were too scared to fight for it. Nevertheless, awareness of the wider world filtered in. Newspapers from the North written by blacks, such as the *Crisis* and the *Pittsburgh Courier*, were circulated in the South. There were also newspapers in the South written by and for blacks, such as the *Norfolk Journal and Guide*, the *Houston Informer* and the *Louisiana Weekly*. Blacks created their own networks too — they had their own schools, churches, colleges and businesses. They appealed for white help and support with education, and many white charities were prepared to offer assistance within the context of segregation. Black communities raised funds from white groups for improved access to health and hospitals for the black community. Booker T. Washington had started National Negro Health Week in 1915 to focus efforts on this. Robert Moton, the head of the organisation in the 1920s, stated: 'If we die, they die. If we get diseased, they will get diseased, and they know it.'

However, there were limitations to such campaigns and they still did not fundamentally challenge the status quo. This is why the NAACP realised that it needed to focus on the institutions that denied equal opportunities to blacks and to target the graduate schools. The organisation had still failed to mount an effective challenge to any of the fundamental obstacles faced by blacks in the South. It had also failed to convince many that it represented the interests of 'ordinary' blacks, and some saw it as an elitist middle-class northern organisation. But to survive in the South the NAACP needed skilled professionals to lead it, as such people were able to retain a degree of independence. In the conditions of the 1930s, lawyers, doctors and church ministers were the only people able to join the NAACP without losing their jobs and livelihoods, although some other black groups enjoyed a degree of autonomy and were able to organise to defend their interests. Blacks in federal employment enjoyed some protection from arbitrary sackings and were also well paid. Black postal workers formed an elite labour group within the community and were well represented with their own union, the National Alliance of Postal Employees (NAPE). This union had supported the NAACP from the start and so helped give it a wider appeal. The creation of Youth Councils also broadened the NAACP's membership — its director of branches was Ella Baker, who would become a key figure in the 1950s. It was out of these various factions that the civil rights movement was to grow, but it needed a major cause to unite and mobilise it.

Challenging 'separate but equal'

The various challenges mounted by the NAACP throughout the 1930s and 1940s had helped to raise its profile but had not really broken through any of the major barriers maintained by the segregated system in the South. Its challenges to segregated graduate schools had met with some success, but such victories made little difference to the great majority of blacks living in the South. The NAACP decided to attack segregation more openly, arguing that 'separate but equal' was unconstitutional and contrary to the Fourteenth Amendment. It also decided to challenge the 'separate but equal' judgement on its own terms, arguing that separate could never be equal: to be equal, education (and other areas) had to integrate. Now it was a matter of finding the right case with which to challenge the system. The NAACP realised it had to choose its battleground carefully, and waited to find a case that would allow it to challenge the whole system of educational segregation. The organisation mounted a challenge in South Carolina on behalf of a group of parents led by Harry Briggs, but this was rejected by the federal district judge. The NAACP (as ever) appealed to the Supreme Court, and in the meantime looked for other cases.

An obvious candidate soon appeared. Linda Brown, who lived in Topeka, Kansas, had to travel across town to a black school, while there was a good white school only seven blocks away. Her father, a minister, had tried to enrol her here but had been turned away. He approached the local NAACP branch for help. The NAACP backed the case and sent two lawyers, Robert Carter and Jack Greenberg, to prepare the case. Little did they realise that this would become one of the defining moments in the civil rights struggle. In *Brown* v *Board of Education of Topeka* the NAACP's counsel Thurgood Marshall challenged the whole system of school segregation. The case was finally heard in December 1952, the Brown case having been amalgamated with other challenges being mounted by the NAACP against segregation — *Briggs* v *Clarendon County*, already mentioned, and *Davis* v *County School Board of Prince Edward County*, challenging segregation in Virginia. A further two more cases were added: *Bolling* v *Sharpe* (challenging segregation at the John Philip Sousa junior high school in Washington, DC) and *Gebhart* v *Belton* (challenging segregation in Delaware).

All five cases would be heard together, which presented a major challenge to Thurgood Marshall, the lawyer arguing the case. He challenged the segregated school system on the grounds that it was unconstitutional and unequal, and the case dragged on as the Supreme Court deliberated for months without coming to a decision. It was again postponed when the principal judge, Chief Justice Vinson, died of a heart attack in September 1953. The new Chief Justice, Earl Warren, was appointed in October and heard a summary of the case in December 1953. He realised that the decision of the Supreme Court would have to be unanimous, and by all accounts he had a challenging time securing it. However, by May 1954 he was ready and on 17 May he gave his verdict. In his judgement he stated that the court could not determine whether the Fourteenth Amendment had aimed to end segregation but that the 'separate but equal' doctrine had been put forward in 1896. Since then times had changed and 'separate but equal' was no longer valid:

> To separate them [blacks] from others of similar age and qualifications solely because of their race generates a feeling of inferiority as to their status in the community that may affect their hearts and minds in a way unlikely ever to be undone.

He went on to say: 'We conclude that, in the field of public education, the doctrine of "separate but equal" has no place. Separate educational facilities are inherently unequal.'

White resistance

The Supreme Court had overturned *Plessy* v *Ferguson* and supported funda-mental change in the South — but the problem was how to implement it. The judgement was greeted with delight by the NAACP, and the black community in the South was heartened, but there remained some serious difficulties. The first was that Chief Justice Warren argued desegregation could be gradual. Second, many state authorities in the South refused to recognise the judgement. Typical of such views was that of the governor of Georgia, Herman Talmadge, who stated that desegregation would result in what he called the 'mongrelisation of the races'. Governor James F. Byrnes of Carolina went further, stating that the end of segregation would 'mark the beginning of the end of civilisation in the South as we have known it'. It was a landmark decision, although the *Washington Post*'s declaration on 19 May that it was a 'new birth of freedom' — a reference to Lincoln's Gettysburg Address — was viewed by many as going too far. It was clear that, as ever, certain parts of the political establishment in the South would mobilise to try to prevent the decision being implemented. The fact that the Supreme Court had ruled that desegregation should proceed with 'all due deliberate speed' gave segregationists the loophole they were looking for. They would simply drag their heels and hope the issue lost its momentum. Oliver Hill, an NAACP lawyer on the *Brown* case, was well aware of this. He said, 'As white folks interpreted it, due deliberate speed meant as long as hell, if any time at all.'

Such deep-rooted resistance to change would be difficult to overcome. James Jackson Kilpatrick, editor the *News Leader* in Richmond, Virginia, succinctly summarised white feelings about segregation when he wrote an article, 'The southern case for school segregation', saying:

In the South, the acceptance of racial separation begins in the cradle. What rational man imagines this concept can be shattered overnight?…The ingrained attitudes of a lifetime cannot be jerked out like a pair of infected molars…Here and now, in his own communities, in the mid-1960s, the Negro race, as a race, plainly is not equal to the white race.

Many would argue that somehow the southern way of life could not coexist with black equality. Others in the South would be subtler, arguing for more time and greater patience. Integration would be gradual but it would come. Many whites who argued this were really using it as a delaying tactic, without ever intending to implement it, as could be seen in the states that resisted segregation over the following decade.

Attitudes were not uniform across the South. Some states moved quickly towards integration, while others remained resolutely opposed and would not give in without a major fight. This became apparent within a year of the *Brown* decision. In this period more than 500 school districts in the South desegregated. In other areas there had been no change. In Georgia, Governor Talmadge stated that there would be no 'mixing of the races in the public schools or any other tax-supported institutions'. In many areas white 'Citizens' Councils' formed to prevent desegregation, and the Ku Klux Klan enjoyed a resurgence as it adopted terror as a tactic against the Supreme Court ruling. In March 1956, 96 southern Congressmen issued a 'Southern Manifesto'. It denounced the *Brown* ruling and called for 'all lawful means' to be employed to 'reverse this decision which is contrary to the Constitution'. The pace of integration began to slow and it was clear that the federal government would have to take further action to force it on a reluctant southern establishment.

This marked the beginning of a pattern in the early years of the civil rights campaign. Local communities in the South would challenge segregation and be met with opposition. They would involve the NAACP, which would try to mount a legal challenge in support of them. This would often end up being referred all the way to the Supreme Court, which on a number of occasions in the 1950s and 1960s supported the challenge. The southern states would then try to resist the Supreme Court ruling with a variety of tactics, mostly delaying ones. This would force the black community and the NAACP to mount further challenges in an attempt to compel the local states to implement the Supreme Court rulings. If this failed they would try to push the situation into one of open conflict, forcing the federal government to intervene in support of the civil rights activists and against the segregationists. These mass mobilisations increased during the 1950s, and then in the 1960s they took on their own life as local community activists mounted spontaneous challenges to the system through actions such as sit-ins and 'freedom rides'. Violent reaction to such actions by police or paramilitary forces was counterproductive, as it forced the federal government to step in to protect activists and undermined the states' powers further. However, this was not always apparent at the time, and many were killed or injured in attempts to achieve this goal.

The wider world

Another important reason for the growing success of the civil rights movement was that the context had changed. The Cold War had brought the USA into conflict with the USSR. This was an ideological as well as a military conflict, in which the USA positioned itself as 'defender of the free world' against a tyrannical opponent, the USSR. The Truman Doctrine had strengthened the USA in its foreign commitments. The doctrine promised American help to countries everywhere as they fought 'internal' and 'external' enemies that wanted to end freedom. America intervened in Greece to support the government against Communist rebels, and also fought the Korean War from 1950 to 1953 to prevent the spread of communism. An important element of this conflict was propaganda, in which the USA had to appear to guarantee freedom. The USSR was also engaged in presenting itself as a defender of both freedom and the workers of the world, and was quick to seize on American treatment of blacks as an example of US hypocrisy. Racial conflict in the USA, it said, was evidence of the fact that the country was not really free but was under the control of powerful capitalist elites who oppressed the poor, and most obviously poor blacks. Southern racism undermined America's moral authority in the eyes of the world, and was a gift to Soviet propagandists.

It was also a world in which new forces were at work, one of the most powerful of which was the media. The growth of cinema, the birth of television and the popularity of all forms of media meant that it was difficult to keep things hidden. The civil rights struggle was good copy. It was an interesting story and it began to attract national and international attention. The birth of youth culture and the growth of a 'counter-culture' also made the civil rights movement a significant contemporary issue. Whites in the North became involved. It was a popular liberal cause, and new activists widened the struggle. As the movement grew, it threw up its own heroes such as Martin Luther King, Malcolm X and Stokely Carmichael, who would appeal to different groups in the black and white communities.

Civil rights activists were quick to realise the power of the media, and those involved in planning the struggle realised that non-violence would be the key to retaining the support of the media and preserving their own moral authority. If they could bring a sense of moral power that was recognisable to everyone to their movement, they would have a much greater chance of success. The involvement of the churches and the strongly religious element in the civil rights struggle would be one of its great strengths, endowing its leaders with a historic sense of mission and generating a huge amount of energy. It is no surprise that leaders within the civil rights movement, especially King, had studied Gandhi's campaign in India against the British and learned valuable lessons that they would bring to America.

Frustration

The abandonment of non-violence from the mid-1960s onwards amid growing frustration at continued economic inequality would fracture the movement and cause it to lose focus. However, success seemed a long way off in 1956, when a ferocious backlash appeared to have successfully stalled the progress of the civil rights movement. The optimism generated by the *Brown* decision had largely dissipated. It became clear that while the Supreme Court might rule segregation unconstitutional, there was still a need for support to push through the implementation of that ruling. In the 2 years that had passed since *Brown*, the federal government had proved reluctant to provide it. President Dwight D. Eisenhower was wary of getting involved in the civil rights movement and did not want to antagonise the South or its politicians in Congress.

The decision of the Supreme Court not to force segregation and instead to allow a year to implement it (a year that ended in May 1955 with the court again failing to impose a deadline) meant that the initial success of the NAACP in the *Brown* case was diluted. The proliferation of the Citizens' Councils further depressed observers. Councils spread throughout the South and by 1956 had over 250,000 members. They threatened activists and ensured that their supporters in the South faced severe economic hardship if they acted openly against segregation. Although there was no clear link between these councils and the Ku Klux Klan, they clearly influenced one another, particularly in creating an atmosphere in which violence could flourish. It looked as if the 1870s might repeat themselves as white segregationists effectively stalled federal government reform. Schools were closed rather than integrated, and private white schools were set up to get round integration. Prince Edward County — named in the original *Brown* decision — kept its schools closed for 8 years. Other states ensured that pupil placement procedures were as complicated and opaque as possible, so that the schools remained segregated. The result of all this activity was that in many places schools did not change at all. This was the case even when it was visibly challenged with federal government support, as happened in the town of Little Rock, Arkansas, in 1957.

The Little Rock Nine

The Little Rock crisis emerged suddenly and was the result of a number of factors. The Little Rock Nine were the only black students that the state of Arkansas was allowing to attend its Central High School in the town of Little Rock. Desegregation in education had become an issue in the preceding year and segregationist feeling had been stirred up by the visit of the governor of Georgia, Marvin Griffin, to Little Rock in August. He stated openly that he was opposed to desegregation in his own state, and advised the citizens of Arkansas likewise to stand firm against the Supreme Court in Little Rock. Battle lines were drawn and it was clear that the nine students were going to attend. The governor of Arkansas, Orval Faubus, appeared before the Chancery Court in Pulaski County, arguing that racial violence was inevitable if black students went to Central High and that people were asking him, 'If Georgia doesn't have to integrate, why does Arkansas have to?' The judge, Chancellor Reed, decided to block integration. A federal district court overturned his decision on 30 August, and Governor Faubus responded by announcing on state television on 2 September that he would deploy the state National Guard to prevent black students attending the school, as he feared 'disorder' might result. The NAACP realised that the stakes in this confrontation were high. If it backed down and allowed Faubus to get away with publicly refusing to integrate, it would have lost a symbolic victory. It would also give new strength to the other states still resisting integration.

On the first day of school, 250 National Guardsmen surrounded Central High and the school board asked that 'no Negro student attempt to attend Central or any white high school until this dilemma is legally resolved'. The next day, the nine students originally enrolled to start school decided to attempt to do so. The NAACP and the federal district court judge, Judge Ronald Davies, had supported them in their decision. He had also told the school board that it could not challenge the students, and its superintendent had told them that they would be allowed to attend. However, when they turned up to school on 4 September an angry mob awaited them and the National Guard refused them entry. It was a stand-off.

The federal government was now the only power that could resolve the issue. Eisenhower was being forced into action and he faced a considerable dilemma. The NAACP had the support of the federal district court and so the president should enforce its decision, but he did not want confrontation with Arkansas and its governor at this time. However, he could hardly ignore such an open statement of defiance. Legal experts argued that the Constitution itself was being tested and that the president must intervene. Faubus flew to Washington to meet the president face to face and promised to resolve the crisis. He undertook to protect the black students and to use the National Guard to maintain order and support integration. Yet he went back on his word, and on 23 September he simply withdrew them. The black students who had finally got into the school had to flee for their lives and there were ugly scenes of violence. Eisenhower, now exasperated by events, interpreted Faubus's actions as insurrection. For Eisenhower, Little Rock was not about race but about the Constitution and the integrity of the Union. He stated:

If we have to do this, and I don't see any alternative, then let's apply the best military principles to it and see that the force we send there is strong enough that it will not be challenged, and will not result in any clash.

By the morning of 25 September there were 1,000 soldiers from the 101st Airborne Division deployed around the school to maintain order. The Little

Rock Nine were finally able to attend school. Despite a continued military presence, the Little Rock Nine endured a difficult time at the school. They were the only blacks among 1,900 white peers and suffered constant bullying and humiliation. The effects of this were long-lasting. One, Gloria Ray, later spoke of her ordeal, saying: 'I was hit and kicked and still bear the mental and physical scars.' Another, Elizabeth Beckford, still suffered from a fear of crowds many years later, and believed that she had 'post-traumatic stress disorder because we were knocked about daily at Central. I still can't stand to have people close behind me, even in an elevator.' A third, Melba Pattillo, complained of this bullying to Martin Luther King, who encouraged her to hold firm, telling her she was doing this 'for generations yet unborn'. She later said: 'When I look at what Nelson Mandela did and slaves who revolted, and Rosa Parks, and Gandhi, we are all one.'

All but one of the Nine completed their education at Central and graduated. The Little Rock crisis was important for a number of reasons, both positive and negative. The federal government had intervened to support civil rights (though only under extreme pressure) and the NAACP seemed to have won a victory. However, white segregationists responded by closing schools to resist segregation so that blacks continued to be shut out of white schools for the next few years (this finally ended in 1959 when it was declared unconstitutional). Governor Faubus was also re-elected, which showed that his stance in 1957 had reinforced his popularity even if it had failed to prevent defeat. In fact his actions had, as Taylor Branch notes, 'brought international ridicule down upon his state'. It was clear that the struggle would be a long one, and that segregationists would resist integration fiercely. The episode also demonstrated that the role of the federal government and the president would be crucial. By the end of the 1950s fewer than 1% of black students in the South would be enrolled in desegregated schools (5 years after the Supreme Court ruled that desegregation was illegal), but the long-term significance of the Little Rock crisis was undeniable. The Little Rock Nine inspired others to challenge the segregated system in the South. All nine were awarded the Congressional Gold Medal in 1999 by President Bill Clinton and were also invited as honoured guests to President Barack Obama's inauguration ceremony in Washington in January 2009. In fact Melba Pattillo said that Obama had previously told her 'that he aspired to climb the steps of the White House because the Little Rock Nine climbed the steps of Central High School'.

In the short term, though, segregationists still refused to accept black students in schools and universities. This was made clear in 1962 when James Meredith tried to enrol at the all-white University of Mississippi in Oxford. A federal district court had ruled that James Meredith must be admitted to the university.

Once again a politician enjoying diminishing popularity made a stand to increase his prestige: Governor Ross Barnett refused to allow him to attend. As negotiations with President Kennedy stalled, the president deployed troops to force the university to allow Meredith to attend, and riots erupted on the campus on the night of 30 September. As violence spread, the president was forced to send in more soldiers and fierce fighting followed. By the time order was restored, 28 federal marshals had been injured, two men were dead and 200 people had been arrested. However, James Meredith attended the university and graduated in the summer of 1963. Once again segregationists had failed to prevent a black student attending a previously all-white institution and once again the federal government had intervened decisively to force change. Further progress followed over the next decade; in 1969 the Supreme Court ruled in the *Alexander* v *Holmes County Board of Education* case that desegregation should proceed immediately and no further delays would be tolerated. Between 1969 and 1974 the proportion of black schoolchildren in the Old South being educated in segregated schools dropped from 68% to 8%. Nevertheless, in 1971 segregation was still common in other areas in America, owing to the fact that housing was often divided along racial lines.

Questions

1 What were the limitations of the NAACP's strategy for challenging segregation?
2 Why did *Brown* v *Board of Education, Topeka* fail to end school segregation?
3 How did the Little Rock crisis transform the strategy of civil rights campaigners in the South?

Chapter 5

How did the civil rights struggle become a mass movement?

Although attempts to force the desegregation of education had achieved considerable press attention and had been popular with the wider black community, they had not mobilised large numbers of blacks. The issue that would eventually achieve this was more mundane, but its impact on blacks was more direct. This was the issue of segregation on transport. Segregation in all areas of life was normal in the South. There were separate restaurants, entertainment facilities, toilets and transport. Segregation on public transport was quite difficult to enforce, however, as it was not possible to have completely separate transport: blacks and whites had to sit on the same bus or train, so they were forced to sit in separate areas. On buses a rather complex protocol governed where the different races sat. The simple rule was that blacks sat at the back and whites at the front, and that blacks then had to give up their seat to any whites left standing.

Blacks had challenged this on numerous occasions, particularly in the Second World War. In Birmingham, Alabama, there had been more than 55 incidents in 1941–42 in which blacks had defied white drivers and refused to move or give up their seats. In New Orleans in 1943, 24 blacks were arrested in one incident after refusing to move. In 1944, Sarah Morris Davis filed an unsuccessful lawsuit against Virginia's segregation law after being arrested and fined for refusing to move. Two black soldiers were even shot in separate incidents by white drivers after refusing to move from particular seats. However, despite these frequent incidents, transport in the South remained segregated and the buses continued to be divided into 'white' and 'coloured' sections.

There had also been a long-running argument between advocates of direct action and those who favoured a more gradualist, legalistic approach. Certain civil rights campaigners argued that segregation would have to be challenged more assertively than in the courts. To some extent the NAACP embodied the cautious approach to civil rights, whereas other organisations such as CORE were more radical. This split had been clear in 1947, when CORE had proposed its Journey of Reconciliation. The first attempt at a 'freedom ride' had been criticised by the NAACP, which argued it was too dangerous. Thurgood Marshall, head of the NAACP's legal department, was strongly against the Journey of Reconciliation and warned that a 'disobedience movement on the part of Negroes and their white allies, if employed in the South, would result in wholesale slaughter with no good achieved'. The Journey of Reconciliation did not lead to such dire consequences, but it failed to mobilise mass support or put segregation under much strain.

By the mid-1950s, however, the political landscape was changing and the NAACP, although still cautious, was opening up to the idea of mass action to challenge segregation. It was also increasingly focused on public transport as one of the most visible symbols of a divided South.

Montgomery bus boycott and the birth of direct action

Montgomery, the state capital of Alabama, was the scene of the first mass mobilisation of the black community in the South against segregation. The transport system in Montgomery was segregated (as in much of the South) and also relied for much of its custom on the black community. NAACP leaders were aware that if they could organise a boycott of the transport system in such a city in response to the arrest of someone for violating the segregation laws, they could force that transport company to desegregate. Ed Nixon, a local community leader, was determined to organise an effective campaign against segregation on public transport. He was the Montgomery representative of the Brotherhood of Sleeping Car Porters (which had been active in securing better pay deals in the 1930s and 1940s) and also a local leader in the NAACP. He would be aided by the emergence of a local church minister, Martin Luther King, who would lead the eventual boycott. It was now a case of waiting for the right case around which they could rally their supporters.

An important factor in determining the suitability of such a case was the defendant's character and profile. The NAACP adopted its normal tactic of trying to find a case to support in which the black litigant was above reproach, so that he or she could not be portrayed in a negative way by lawyers defending segregation. This approach meant that some challengers to segregation on public transport were not supported. Claudette Colvin was one such example. A 15-year-old black girl, she was thrown off a bus in Montgomery 9 months before Rosa Parks in almost exactly the same circumstances. She too pleaded not guilty to breaking the law and she also soon gathered support from the local black community, which prepared to mobilise national support. Unfortunately, she fell pregnant just as the campaign was gathering pace and was quickly deemed unsuitable by the male, middle-class and churchgoing black leadership in Montgomery. Rosa Parks was a more suitable candidate for support. She herself acknowledged this, saying: 'If the white press got ahold of that information, they would have had a field day. They'd call her a bad girl, and her case wouldn't have had a chance.' Ed Nixon supported this:

Mrs Parks was a married woman. She was morally clean and she had a fairly good academic training…If there was ever a person we would've been able to use to break the situation that existed on the Montgomery city line, Rosa L. Parks was the woman to use…I probably would've examined a dozen more before I got there if Rosa Park's hadn't come along before I found the right one.

Another woman, Mary Louise Smith, was also arrested in the same period but Nixon claimed her father was a drunkard and refused to take up her case.

Thus it was that history was made when Mrs Rosa Parks refused to give up her seat and move to the back of the bus when ordered to do so by the driver, James F. Blake, in Montgomery, Alabama, on 1 December 1955. Ed Nixon paid her bail and quickly mobilised the community in support. Rosa Parks had been the secretary of the Montgomery chapter of the NAACP and was still involved with its youth association. She was thoroughly respectable and an ideal figurehead for a campaign against segregation. Nixon decided to use a boycott of the buses to force change. This was not a novel idea. In the town of Baton Rouge, Louisiana, there had been two bus boycotts in 1953, one of which had lasted a week and had forced the city officials to offer a compromise on segregated seating to local black leaders.

In Montgomery, within 24 hours of Rosa Parks' arrest local activists were handing out leaflets highlighting the injustice of her case, and within a week the boycott was underway. Nixon had realised that one way of effecting change was to hit businesses where it hurt — in their wallets. As blacks accounted for over 75% of the Montgomery bus company's customers, a successful boycott could force a change in policy. The bus boycott was carefully planned: leaflets were issued spreading the word, while public meetings cemented the message and united the black community. The boycott, which began on 5 December, was timed to coincide with Rosa Parks' appearance in court. It was an instant success, and over 90% of the city's 40,000 blacks stayed off the buses. Rosa Parks became a celebrity, an iconic figure of the civil rights movement. She was on the receiving committee that met Nelson Mandela in 1990 in Detroit and is remembered by history as one of the pioneers of the civil rights struggle. Troy State University opened its Rosa Parks museum in 2000 in Montgomery to honour the town's role in the struggle.

Martin Luther King

While Rosa Parks emerged as an icon of the civil rights movement, the Montgomery bus boycott also created another hero: Martin Luther King. A local minister in the Dexter Avenue Baptist Church, Martin Luther King was well placed to take a leadership role in the boycott. He was charismatic, well educated and respectable. It is also no accident that he was a minister. As Manning Marable wrote in his book *Black Leadership*:

> The principal social institution within every black community was the church. As political leaders, the black clergy were usually the primary spokespersons for the entire black community, especially during periods of crisis…To some extent this tradition has been characterised by a charismatic or dominating political style.

This tradition helped create what he called a 'black messianic style' that has defined much of the civil rights leadership over the last 60 years. Martin Luther King, Malcolm X and Jesse Jackson all shared elements of this. They combined the roles of politician and preacher and were often treated as visionaries — extraordinary leaders who commanded total obedience. The 'cults' that can grow up around such leaders could often frustrate others in the movement. King could inspire resentment as well as love. What was clear from an early stage in the Montgomery bus boycott was that here was a local leader who could inspire national attention, and in a media age he was an ideal 'face' for the masses to identify with.

The church had been the focus for black autonomy and resistance since slavery, and Martin Luther King was born into a tradition of preaching and religious faith. But churches in the South were much more than places of worship — they were centres of education and support. They raised large sums of money and were the one place where blacks could meet free from intimidation. It is not surprising that in the segregated South the churches attracted the brightest and best. Church leaders had a huge amount of power in the local black community. They were its elite, its leaders, and in a society that denied them many opportunities the job of minister was one of the only routes to success. The fact that so many of the civil rights movement's leaders were ministers gave it enormous legitimacy and linked it to other churches across the globe. The religious element of the civil rights movement was essential to its success. In the age of the mass media, state violence against blacks was increasingly unacceptable, and this was even more true when they were religious leaders. The civil rights movement was well aware of this from the start.

Martin Luther King became a minister after completing a degree at Crozer Theological Seminary in Chester, Pennsylvania, and a doctorate at Boston University. A liberal and forward-thinking institute, Crozer had allowed King to develop his own ideas about religion and encouraged progressive thought. Although it was predominantly a white college there were plenty of black students, as well as others from China, India and other countries. Historian Taylor Branch writes: 'No major seminary of any denomination had achieved such a racial mix, and none would do so ever again, even after the black revolution of the next generation.' King had quickly established himself as an effective public speaker. As Branch notes: 'King's oratory was among his chief distinctions at Crozer. His peers so admired his preaching technique that they packed the chapel whenever he delivered the regular Thursday student sermon.' After completing his studies, King became minister at Dexter Avenue Baptist Church in Montgomery, Alabama, in April 1954. At this stage there was no real indication that he would take a prominent role in the civil rights movement, and not much indication that he was preoccupied with the issue. However, when the bus boycott began he clearly believed that it was justified, and his personal convictions and religious beliefs motivated his decision to get heavily involved in the movement. During the events of 1955–56 he became well known at the national and international level as he assumed leadership of the organisation formed to manage the boycott: the Montgomery Improvement Association (MIA).

Maintaining the boycott proved to be hard work. Initially, it was only supposed to last a single day, but a public meeting at Holt Street Baptist Church at the end of the first day showed the mood was not for compromise. Martin Luther King stirred the crowd with a speech demanding change and eschewing violence. He said:

> One of the great glories of democracy is the right to protest for right…If you will protest courageously and yet with dignity and Christian love, when the history books are written in future generations the historians will pause and say, 'There lived a great people — a black people — who injected new meaning and dignity into the veins of civilisation.'

King cleverly linked the civil rights movement with the cause of democracy and freedom that America believed it was defending in the Cold War. He was always patriotic and his refusal to engage in or support violence meant that he retained the moral high ground. The strongly religious nature of his worldview also won him support in a firmly Christian society. Most importantly, he presented the black struggle for civil rights as one in which they were simply asking for the entitlement guaranteed them by the US Constitution, both in its original spirit and also in its Fourteenth and Fifteenth Amendments.

At the end of the meeting on the first day of the boycott the majority vote was to continue it until three demands had been met. The first was for courteous treatment on the buses. The second was for first-come-first-served seating, with whites at the front and blacks at the back. The third was for black bus drivers to be hired on black routes. These demands were hardly revolutionary and stopped short of full integration, but the city officials refused to negotiate on them when they met. The continuation of the boycott became a national story and then an international one. Martin Luther King's charisma helped push the story into the public eye and keep it there, but what really impressed onlookers was the unity and determination of the black community.

However, the boycott continued to face many challenges. Black taxi drivers were told they had to charge full fares or be prosecuted, as part of the authorities' attempt to force passengers back onto the buses. When a transportation committee set up by the Montgomery Improvement Association started to organise a car pool, its drivers were harassed by the police and fined for various infractions. There was more serious violence too — King's house was bombed, and so was Ed Nixon's. On 21 February 1956, 29 ministers, including King, were indicted for conspiring to boycott; at the subsequent trial King was punished with a fine of $500 and court costs, or 386 days of hard labour. The MIA countered with a lawsuit challenging the constitutionality of segregation and won its suit on 2 June, but the city commissioners appealed the federal district court's decision and the case went on to be heard by the Supreme Court. In the meantime the boycott continued. The matter came to a head on 13 November, when the Supreme Court ruled that segregation was unconstitutional. The segregationists challenged the ruling on the grounds that it violated states' rights, but the Supreme Court stood firm and the written mandate enforcing the ruling arrived on 20 December. The protracted struggle had exhausted both sides and many whites were secretly glad that it was over, as business had suffered during the boycott. The bus company had also suffered, nearing bankruptcy. Transport in Montgomery was completely desegregated from 21 December 1956.

Non-violence

As well as producing the most notable figure of the civil rights movement, the bus boycott in Montgomery had created its most effective tactic — that of non-violence. Non-violence had not been an inevitable option for the civil rights movement, and there were instances during the boycott (for example after the bombing of Martin Luther King's house) when it looked as if angry blacks would decide to attack police officers. But Martin Luther King publicly embraced the philosophy of non-violence early on in the boycott and violence was avoided. King was instinctively in favour of non-violence but was relatively naïve regarding how to ensure it remained a guiding principle in tense and potentially violent times. A key figure who helped him was Bayard Rustin, a veteran civil rights campaigner who had arrived in Montgomery during the boycott and was instantly attracted by the atmosphere and spirit of the protest. Despite major differences, the two men quickly established a rapport. Rustin felt that King and the other leaders of the MIA were unschooled in non-violence and needed support but was aware that his own background in Communist and labour agitation could discredit the campaign. Glen Smiley, another veteran pacifist, replaced him. In fact, it was Glen Smiley who boarded a bus with Martin Luther King on 21 December 1956 and signalled the end of the boycott.

The civil rights movement's attachment to non-violence would be one of the keys to its success, as it gave the various groups involved in the struggle a clear modus operandi and moral strength that helped them resist the violence they faced with dignity and calm. As time passed, the theory and practice of non-violent action became more refined, and workshops would school budding activists in how to maintain non-violence under pressure. Initially, though, it was instinctive. When James Lawson, an experienced pacifist, met Martin Luther King in February 1957 he realised that he and King were essentially on the same wavelength. Lawson had spent time in India studying the actions of Mahatma Gandhi and his organisation of effective protest against British rule in India in the 1930s. He had also been imprisoned for refusing to join the army in 1951 and had been attracted to the civil rights movement from the start. He would work with King from 1957 until King's murder in Memphis in 1968.

Montgomery also marked the birth of a mass civil rights movement. There can be no doubt that Martin Luther King was essential in giving the movement mass appeal. He gave it the charismatic figurehead that it had lacked until that stage — he helped move it out of the courtroom and the control of the NAACP and onto the streets. He was also popular with the press and a great orator. His religious conviction made him a tremendously inspiring figure who gave people the sense that they were taking part in an epic moral battle and that supporting him was the right thing to do. He was a truly extraordinary man, whose religious convictions and humanitarian worldview offered the blacks a sense of vision that would help them stake everything on victory and overcome the wave of violence and oppression that their struggle would bring down on them.

Once the boycott was over, Martin Luther King was keen to build on the achievements and continue to advance the cause of black freedom in the South but he was unsure how to go about it. The Supreme Court had decreed that segregation on public transport was unconstitutional and ordered the states to integrate schools, but local governments were still dragging their feet and trying to block change. In states like Georgia and Mississippi, little changed: blacks were still denied the vote and segregation was still a fact of life. King realised that the movement for civil rights needed to reach a critical mass so that the South would be forced to change. King also realised that mass action would be the key to achieving that change and that he would have to force the federal government to get involved. It would be a difficult task: Montgomery had shown that it could be done, but it was now a case of building the momentum to keep change coming.

The question was what to do next: how should blacks keep up the pressure to end segregation? On 13 June 1957 King met Vice-President Richard Nixon to discuss the race issue. King requested direct presidential support for deseg-regation in the South and Nixon promised a new civil rights bill. After much debate and some amendment the Civil Rights Act was passed in August 1957, but it achieved little. It empowered the Justice Department to initiate lawsuits in voting rights cases and also set up a civil rights commission to investigate violations of the law. A second Act, passed in 1960, aimed to strengthen federal powers to enforce voter registration but again the provisions were so watered down that they achieved little. Martin Luther King and Roy Wilkins, executive secretary of the NAACP, were fairly non-committal in their support, although some in the civil rights movement believed that any legislation was better than none. Overall, though, the Republican President Eisenhower had disappointed the leaders of the civil rights movement and proved reluctant to act effectively on the issue. The pendulum now swung away from central government and back to 'people power', as 1960 saw the sit-in movement spread across the South.

The sit-in movement

The sit-in movement marked a new phase in the civil rights struggle. After the Montgomery bus boycott, Martin Luther King had emerged as the public face of the civil rights struggle. In January 1957 the Southern Christian Leadership Conference (SCLC) was founded in an attempt to capitalise on the actions in Montgomery of the previous year. It consisted mainly of black ministers and linked the civil rights movement clearly to the religious establishment in the South. It preached non-violent direct action to end segregation. It was a southern movement and was based on the black church. The SCLC therefore differed greatly from the NAACP, which was northern, secular and regarded as overly influenced by white members. The SCLC had no membership lists, was loosely organised and could avoid the overt legal challenges the NAACP had faced from Citizens' Councils and other segregationist groups. Its leadership comprised many prominent black ministers who were also involved in civil rights. C. K. Steele had led a bus boycott in Tallahassee, Florida, while Fred L. Shuttlesworth was leader of the Alabama Christian Movement for Human Rights. However, the dominant figure in the group was Martin Luther King. He also used northern supporters such as Glen Smiley and James Lawson to help plan strategy. They were prominent in the Fellowship of Reconciliation (FOR), which ran workshops on non-violent direct action on southern campuses.

The civil rights movement at the time began attracting a younger generation of students and activists. Some of them were based in the North and some in the South. Diane Nash, a student at Fisk University, and John Lewis, a student at the American Baptist Theological Seminary in Nashville, were typical of this new generation. Inspired by the Montgomery bus boycott and having attended workshops run by FOR, they helped set up the Nashville Student Movement and decided to target segregation in the city. While they were deciding the best ways to challenge segregation, four black students from the Agricultural and Technical College in Greensboro, North Carolina, beat them to it. They staged a sit-in at the lunch counter of the local F. W. Woolworth store. The four students — Joseph McNeil, Ezell Blair Jnr, Franklin McCain and David Richmond — had all been involved in their local NAACP youth group and had planned their action carefully. When they took their seats at the white-only lunch counter on 1 February 1960 a newspaper reporter was on hand to record the event and the four were expecting to inspire copycat actions across the South. The next day 29 other students joined the action, and within 5 days there were hundreds more, with the activists also targeting the S. H. Kress store in the same street. This was a genuine grass-roots movement to target segregation, which challenged it directly and spread rapidly.

The sit-in movement sparked by the four young men from the A&T College in Greensboro was not original. The tactic had been tried before by CORE in Chicago and Baltimore in 1952 and by the NAACP in 1958 in Oklahoma, but this was different. The spontaneous nature of the protest and the fact that the students were acting alone, without the approval of NAACP or CORE or any other organisation, gave the protests their own dynamic. Within days there were hundreds of protesters. The sit-in tactics spread quickly across the South. One of the original protesters, Franklin McCain, explained their motivation:

> We were all Christians and we took our motivation from this man called Jesus…Then there was Gandhi, who kicked the hell out of the British…We had to be non-violent because we didn't have the bodies and we didn't have the guns. We could not have got the endorsement either, if we had resorted to violence.

However, if the actions of the Greensboro students and those who followed had been spontaneous, it was quickly apparent to more senior members in the movement that the sit-ins sweeping the South could help the wider civil rights struggle find new energy and direction. Black people were now taking the struggle onto the streets of southern cities, into white spaces that had hitherto been out of bounds to them, and so were directly challenging the segregationist system. They were playing a dangerous game. It would involve them in direct conflict with the police and other authorities. More than 3,600 students would be arrested in 1960 alone for public order offences and 'breaches of the peace', the charges generally brought by the police against such demonstrators. The young students involved in the protests were less vulnerable to such threats than older activists. They did not have families to support and were able to play the 'jail not bail' card that helped clog up the jail system and put additional pressure on law enforcement agencies. The black community also rallied round its activists and helped raise bail money and encouraged them to continue. Thurgood Marshall and the NAACP backed the campaign, as did many university authorities. The movement received generally positive coverage in the media in the North: it was difficult to dislike the sober, earnest and Christian protesters and easy to despise the baying mobs that were attacking them.

Various organisations emerged at the time to help coordinate this new wave of actions. Ella Baker, the SCLC's executive director, was soon contacting universities across the South to encourage students to take direct action. The sit-ins spread. In Tallahassee and New Orleans black and white students together challenged segregation in restaurants, and all across the South the movement gathered pace. The *New York Times* said at the end of February that 'the movement has spread from North Carolina, to Virginia, Florida, South Carolina, and Tennessee and involved 15 cities'. In the aftermath of sit-ins students began to protest outside segregated stores, and the ensuing economic damage began to force change. In Nashville sales slumped as the protests frightened whites away and the blacks boycotted the shops, and shopkeepers began to push for a settlement. Other cities also felt the pressure, and in the upper South stores began to desegregate. On 19 March 1960 San Antonio, Texas, became the first city in the South to desegregate its lunch counters. Nashville followed in May, and by 1961 a further 80 towns and cities had also integrated. Students in the North had added to the pressure on national stores such as Woolworth's by picketing them.

The spontaneous and devolved nature of the sit-in protests also challenged the traditional black civil rights leadership. The NAACP had little role in the protests and Martin Luther King was also often out of the loop, because the students were organising themselves — this was a new generation and they wanted to do things their own way. Ella Baker linked the activists to the SCLC leadership and encouraged them to meet on Easter weekend 1960 at Shaw University in Raleigh, North Carolina. It became apparent that the SCLC leadership would not be able to lead them and that they wanted their own organisation: the Student Nonviolent Coordinating Committee (SNCC, pronounced 'snick') was the result.

The SNCC would come to represent the interests of the newer, more radical emerging activists who would help lead the next phase of the struggle. It would also come into conflict with the SCLC and Martin Luther King over the nature and aims of the civil rights movement. In fact, Martin Luther King had agreed to take part in a sit-in on 19 October 1960 in Atlanta, Georgia, to show his support for the movement. He had moved there from Montgomery the previous year in order to lead the SCLC more effectively and found it difficult to refuse requests from activists in the city to join the protests. It was not a step he had taken lightly — he had been arrested before but did not relish confrontation and knew that he would be an obvious target for the police. So it was that on the morning of 19 October King was arrested after entering a restaurant called the Magnolia Room. He refused to pay bail and was jailed along with 35 students. King then found himself jailed for a further 4 months as he had been arrested earlier for driving without a Georgia licence. He faced some hard time at Reidsville State Penitentiary unless someone could get him out. Luckily for him it was election year and both candidates wanted to prove their civil rights credentials with as little cost to themselves as possible. John Kennedy was standing for the Democrats and Richard Nixon was the Republican candidate. Kennedy called King's wife, Coretta Scott. His younger brother, Robert, phoned Judge Oscar Mitchell in Atlanta and the next day King was released on bail. Martin Luther King Senior stated: 'It's time for all of us to take off our Nixon button.' Many blacks switched their support to the Democrats, and in the election of that year over 68% of them voted for Kennedy, 7% more than before. Civil rights had finally become an election issue.

Freedom rides

Next it was the turn of a small and relatively minor faction of the civil rights movement to initiate events. The Congress of Racial Equality (CORE) had been set up in 1943 by a small group of radical proponents of direct action and non-violence to challenge segregation. Their most notable action until 1961 had been organising the Journey of Reconciliation in 1947. A lot had changed between 1947 and 1961, and a recent Supreme Court ruling had given activists hope that segregation on federal transport could be effectively challenged. The *Boynton* v *Commonwealth of Virginia* judgement in December 1960 had ruled it illegal to enforce racial segregation in facilities at bus stations for passengers travelling from one state to another. James Farmer, one of the original founders of CORE and also one of the original travellers on the Journey of Reconciliation, believed that a group of committed activists could force the federal government to support the recent Supreme Court decision by riding federal buses across the South and refusing to respect the segregation laws. The intention was clear. As Farmer stated: 'We felt we could count on the racists of the South to create a crisis so that the federal government would be compelled to enforce the law.' He would be proved correct.

The initial plan was quite simple: a racially mixed group of activists would set out in two groups to travel across the South. One would travel by the Greyhound bus company and the other by Trailways. Blacks would sit in the white areas and vice versa, and at each stop they would use the facilities reserved for the other race. Farmer wrote to the president, the attorney general, the director of the FBI and the transport companies involved to warn them of the action and give them a detailed itinerary. They would start in Washington, DC, and arrive in New Orleans on 17 May 1961. Thirteen 'freedom riders' set off on 4 May. The first few days went without incident and they met Martin Luther King in Atlanta for a meal and some words of encouragement. Both groups left Atlanta on their separate buses to proceed, and from this point onwards violent opposition started. Bayard Rustin's statement that 'protest becomes effective to the extent that it elicits brutality and oppression from the power structure' was to be tested to its limit. James Peck, one of the original members of the 1947 'Journey of Reconciliation', was leader of the Trailways group. Joe Perkins, a CORE field secretary, was leader of the group travelling by Greyhound.

It was Perkins' group who ran into violence first. An angry mob intercepted them in Anniston, Alabama, and set their bus on fire. The freedom riders received a severe beating after escaping from the burning bus and were only saved when a plain-clothes policeman pulled a gun on their attackers. The

Trailways bus made it to Birmingham, where they met a reception committee organised by the Ku Klux Klan. Once again the freedom riders were badly beaten and could easily have been killed. Photos of the attacks were soon front-page news across the world, with the *Daily Mirror* in Britain saying that President Kennedy was now facing one of the supreme tests of his leadership. The Soviet press also covered the beatings, pointing out the obvious gap between vision and reality in the 'land of the free'. The riders decided that in this case discretion was the better part of valour and flew from Birmingham to New Orleans. However, as with the sit-in movement before them, their action inspired others to follow their example, and soon other freedom riders were heading south.

A second group of freedom riders soon set off from Nashville to try to make it further than Peck and co. This time they got to Birmingham but ran into trouble in Montgomery, where they too were seriously assaulted. Martin Luther King flew to Montgomery to give a speech supporting the beaten freedom riders and was joined by James Farmer and Diane Nash (one of the leaders of the SNCC and organiser of the second freedom ride). While King was speaking at the First Baptist Church it was surrounded by an angry white mob who burned cars, hurled bricks and petrol bombs onto the church and began firing shots. Inside the church King contacted the Kennedys to try to galvanise them into action. Eventually the governor of Alabama deployed enough police to protect the congregation and disperse the waiting mob. The Nashville freedom riders were then escorted out of the city by a heavy army presence and arrived at their next destination: Jackson, Mississippi. There they were arrested and sent to prison. More freedom riders followed and over 355 were arrested.

Once again the world's media were focused on the story and once again the success of direct action in challenging segregation and forcing the federal government to act was being demonstrated. Those arrested refused bail in a 'jail not bail' campaign aimed at causing as much trouble as possible for southern police forces. By clogging up the judicial system with defendants and keeping the issue in the public eye, they forced Kennedy to act. On 1 November 1961 the Interstate Commerce Commission (ICC) banned segregation and discrim-ination on interstate travel. The CORE campaign had met with success and forced the federal government to act.

It had not, however, ended segregation in the South. The system was being challenged, but in the Deep South the white segregationists still held power and there were still states that had resisted any attempts to force integration. The most notorious of these was Mississippi, but Georgia and Alabama also remained bastions of white supremacists. There was still much to be done: once again the civil rights movement needed to gather its energies and find more effective ways of challenging segregation. Another series of actions would begin, but this time they would meet with much more success. In fact, between 1963 and 1965 the segregationist system in the South would collapse and the victory of the civil rights movement would come with surprising swiftness.

Questions

1 How did mass mobilisation of the black community in the South succeed in undermining the system of segregation?

2 Why was Martin Luther King so important in the civil rights movement?

3 'The sit-in movement changed the nature of the civil rights movement.' How far do you agree with this point of view?

How did the civil rights movement end segregation?

By the end of 1961 the civil rights movement proved that it could mobilise large sections of the black community in support of its objectives. It also proved that it could effect change — many cities in the South had now desegregated their schools, restaurants and buses. The civil rights movement had also pressured the federal government to intervene in support of desegregation at Little Rock, Arkansas, in 1957 and to support the freedom riders in 1961. However, it had not yet succeeded in pushing the federal government into taking decisive action to end segregation. Campaigners realised that they needed to press harder and continue to force change. There was no clear plan of action, but broadly speaking the civil rights leaders and activists decided on a number of different actions. First, they would continue to force confrontation with racist state authorities by direct action and protest. Second, they would try to encourage blacks to register to vote in regions where they were traditionally excluded. Third, they would continue to put pressure on the president to push through effective legislation to guarantee their freedom to vote. These actions would not necessarily be coordinated, but over the next few years the combination of these various tactics would meet with success.

Direct action 1: Albany, Georgia

In the summer of 1961 Albany, Georgia, had become the focus of the civil rights movement. The SNCC decided that it was time to combine all its various methods of protest and focus them on one town to force change. It would flood the city with activists and engage in demonstrations and marches, while also encouraging local blacks to vote. The SNCC was a grass-roots organisation and it encouraged local people to participate as much as possible in the actions. On 17 November various groups came together to form the Albany Movement, an umbrella organisation to coordinate the protests. The NAACP and the SNCC continued to squabble over policy but the public protests carried on. Black activists targeted the segregated bus terminal, freedom riders rode into the city, and school students marched in protest at the arrests of previous protesters. By December 1961 Albany was becoming national news and attracted the support of Martin Luther King, who was soon arrested after taking part in a march to the city hall. However, the attempts by the civil rights campaigners in Albany to provoke headline-grabbing reaction from the city authorities were frustrated by the chief of police, Laurie Pritchett. He avoided overt oppression of the protesters, while still managing to arrest hundreds of them and send them to county jails across the state. He was a formidable adversary. As Juan Williams wrote: 'The Albany Movement watched Pritchett with the grudging admiration of a chicken farmer for a sly fox.'

Despite the best attempts of the civil rights movement, the Albany campaign fizzled out. In some ways it has even been seen as a defeat for the civil rights movement. However, valuable lessons had been learned about how to run a similar campaign. In particular, the importance of careful planning was evident, and it was clear that in future the targets of the movement would have to be more carefully chosen. Pritchett had shown that by avoiding overt oppression and police brutality it was possible to sit out the protests and maintain a segregated system. He admitted that he had studied King's methods carefully and planned his response accordingly. He did not run out of jail space for those arrested and he avoided the negative publicity that heavy-handed police responses would cause. King was forced to abandon his support for the campaign in August 1962 after the local federal judge ordered an end to the demonstrations. The ruling of the federal court meant that Martin Luther King was reluctant to continue protesting. He appealed to Kennedy to intervene in support of the movement. Kennedy refused to do so and Martin Luther King moved on: the Albany Movement continued without him.

Direct action 2: Birmingham, Alabama

Soon after the Albany protests, the SCLC was invited to Birmingham, Alabama, by Fred Shuttlesworth, a black activist who had been fighting for change in the city for years. Birmingham had a population of over 350,000 and was Alabama's largest city. Although blacks made up 40% of the population, they were denied any opportunity to integrate; segregation was entrenched in every municipal institution. The average annual income for blacks was $3,000, less than half that of white workers, and violence against them was common. The Ku Klux Klan was a powerful presence in the city and the police department turned a blind eye to its activities. The first freedom riders had been badly beaten in the city in 1961, and it was notorious as a place where blacks were routinely subjected to discrimination.

Attempts within the white community to end the segregationists' hold on the city had led to new elections that had created an opportunity to get rid of the existing police chief, 'Bull' Connor, but he was refusing to go. As efforts to sort out the electoral chaos continued, the city was effectively being run by two administrations. The SCLC decided to target Birmingham in January 1963 and planned its campaign to start in March. In the meantime it raised funds and prepared the ground, choosing the 16th Street Baptist Church as its headquarters. Martin Luther King made sure he planned carefully: in Albany his plans had effectively been hijacked by events. Birmingham would be different: this time the movement would be prepared. Protests began in April and continued for several weeks. The tactics were familiar — segregated stores were targeted and picketed, and there were marches on the city hall and other institutions.

On 12 April Martin Luther King was arrested and sent to jail. The letter that he wrote from prison attempted to explain and justify the civil rights movement's tactics and philosophy to sceptical local black ministers. Originally a series of notes scrawled on a newspaper, King's letter was later published as a pamphlet and distributed widely. In it he outlined his personal beliefs on equality but also explained the tactics of the movement. He wrote:

> You may well ask, 'Why direct action? Why sit-ins, marches and so forth? Isn't negotiation a better path?' You are quite right in calling for negotiation. Indeed, this is the very purpose of direct action. Non-violent direct action seeks to create such a crisis and foster such a tension that a community which has constantly refused to negotiate is forced to confront the issue. It seeks so to dramatize the issue that it can no longer be ignored…For years now I have heard the word 'Wait!' It rings in the ears of every Negro with piercing familiarity. This 'Wait' has almost always meant 'Never'. We must come to see, with one of our distinguished jurists, that 'justice too long delayed is justice denied'. We have waited for more than 340 years for our constitutional and God-given rights.

King was clear in his strategy: he needed to force confrontation and mobilise first local and then national opinion. If 'Bull' Connor played a similar game to Pritchett, the protests could again peter out and lose momentum. In fact, through April they began to do so. At this stage James Bevel, an experienced activist from the sit-in movement, suggested switching tactics. He decided to mobilise a group hitherto ignored by the movement: schoolchildren. Bevel wanted to get the black community in Birmingham involved in the civil rights movement, and he realised one of the most effective ways of doing so was to get their children involved. There were also other reasons for mobilising children. It required the same resources to arrest and process them as it did adults, they had less to lose, and they were more prepared to take risks. They also believed that what they were doing was worthwhile: they were practising non-violent direct action to achieve equality for their people. On Thursday 2 May groups of children began marching, and by the end of the day 956 had been arrested. The following day over 1,000 more were marching, and finally the civil rights movement in Birmingham got the confrontation and the ensuing publicity that it needed. Ron Field wrote:

> Eugene 'Bull' Connor fell for the bait and countered the young protesters with fire hoses and police dogs. Televised images of children being water hosed, beaten and arrested had a profound impact — not just on the American public but on the rest of the world.

As violence threatened to escalate, a solution became imperative and both sides were eager to move towards a deal that would end the protests. On 10 May the deal was done. It was agreed that lunch counters would be desegregated, blacks would be employed in downtown stores and prisoners released. The truce was condemned by 'Bull' Connor, who spoke of 'weak-kneed white people' giving in to the 'rabble-rouser King', but there was little he could do. On 11 May the Ku Klux Klan also met outside the city to condemn King; the motel where he had been staying was bombed the same night. But King had already left, and in his absence there were outbreaks of violence between angry black crowds and the police. It was becoming harder to ignore the possibility of black violence. Non-violence had worked in the campaign so far, but it had not always been easy to avert confrontations. By 1963 there were signs that the consensus was breaking down among the black community. Martin Luther King had recognised this, warning that 'millions of Negroes' could be forced to 'seek solace and security in black nationalist ideologies, a development that will lead inevitably to a frightening racial nightmare'. The leader of the NAACP in Philadelphia, Cecil Moore, had spoken of his 'basic strength' being dependent on 'lower-class guys who are ready to mob, rob, steal and kill'. Malcolm X, the popular Nation of Islam leader, was also threatening blood-curdling consequences for the white community if the oppression of blacks continued.

The possibility of the civil rights movement falling into the hands of extremists worried President Kennedy and encouraged him to take steps to try to resolve the issues that so angered the blacks. In fact, the president found it increasingly difficult not to get involved as disorder spread in the aftermath of the negotiated end to the Birmingham demonstrations. He sent federal troops to Fort McClellan, 30 miles outside Birmingham, and threatened to intervene if the state government could not restore order. A new mayor, Albert Boutwell, agreed to honour the negotiated agreement and saw order restored. Unfortunately for Kennedy, just as the Birmingham protests were subsiding trouble again flared in Alabama, when Governor George Wallace blocked integration of the state university. On 21 May a federal judge had ordered the university to admit two black students, Vivian Malone and James Hood. George Wallace, like 'Bull' Connor and Orval Faubus, had used the segregation issue to increase his popularity with the white electorate the year before, declaring, 'Segregation now! Segregation tomorrow! Segregation forever!' and on 11 June he refused to allow the black students to enter the university. This time Kennedy was in no mood for compromise and ordered the Alabama National Guard to get the students into the university: they were admitted the same day. That night Kennedy spoke on national television of a 'moral crisis' in the country and promised 'legislation giving all Americans the right to be served in facilities which are open to the public — hotels, restaurants, theatres, retail stores and similar establishments. This seems to me to be an elementary right.' This was the clearest signal yet from the federal government that it was preparing to put its weight behind the movement.

Direct action 3: the March on Washington

In the light of Kennedy's statement the decision by leaders of the civil rights movement to go ahead with a planned march on Washington might have seemed perverse. It certainly seemed so to President Kennedy and his brother Robert, the attorney general. They had just promised to try to deliver a new civil rights bill to Congress on 19 June that would outlaw segregation in all interstate public accommodation, push ahead desegregation in schools and help blacks vote. They consequently felt that the civil rights movement should give them something in return and not stir up more potential trouble. In fact, the Kennedys had opposed the march from the first moment it had been mooted.

However, Martin Luther King had decided to support the march in the aftermath of the Birmingham campaign and met other civil rights leaders on 22 June 1963 when plans for the march were already underway. It had been the long-held dream of one of the fathers of the civil rights movement, Philip Randolph, to hold such a march. He had threatened one in 1941, and this threat had helped secure Executive Order 8802 from President Franklin Roosevelt. Martin Luther King, the SCLC, CORE, SNCC and the NAACP felt that a huge public display of support for integration would help push the bill through and stop it being watered down in the way so many other bills had been. Kennedy's request that Randolph call off the march had been met with the comment, 'the Negroes are already on the streets', and it went ahead. King agreed that the march might be 'ill-timed' but stated that he had 'never engaged in a direct action movement that did not seem ill-timed'.

Kennedy was forced to accept the march and, as Gary Younge points out, he decided that he would try to co-opt what he could not cancel. He declared his support for the march, hailing it as a 'peaceful assembly for the redress of grievances'. It was fortunate for everyone concerned that the march was a triumph. It was peaceful and well organised, and showed the civil rights movement at its best. Despite the Pentagon putting 19,000 troops on standby and preparing for widespread violence there were only four arrests on the day itself — all white people. On 28 August 1963 more than 200,000 people marched in the capital, passing peacefully in front of the White House to gather at the Lincoln memorial. Speeches by leaders of the SNCC and the SCLC emphasised racial unity and harmony. Martin Luther King's speech was the last of the day and has become one of his best known. It was based on a speech he had given several times before in which he imagined a world where race no longer decided a person's fate. His 'I have a dream' speech was broadcast across the nation and once again managed to summarise succinctly many recurring themes that inspired the civil rights activists. His closing statement, expressing the desire that the blacks might enjoy the same rights as all other Americans and become 'free at last', was a sentiment echoed by many.

The March on Washington was a resounding success. Hundreds of thousands had marched peacefully in support of the civil rights movement and shown their support for its aims. But the events of one August day could not change the system alone and decisive action from central government was still required. Despite the success of the March on Washington there was continued violence across the South that summer. Demonstrations in Shreveport, Louisiana, Gadsden, Alabama, and Jackson, Mississippi, were brutally suppressed, often with more violence than in Birmingham. However, although there was still violence, it was apparent that the segregated system could not continue to operate in the face of such widespread disobedience. It was a system that had survived through fear and intimidation but also because historic tradition had persuaded the majority of blacks to accept it. Once large enough numbers of local blacks began to challenge it, its days were numbered. As Martin Luther King stated: '1963 is not an end but a beginning' — the beginning of the end for segregation. This was America, not Nazi Germany: the authorities still had to respect the general spirit of the law, even if they could abuse it to some extent.

The federal government had also demonstrated that it would not stand by and watch wholesale chaos. There would be no massacres — the state governments of the South could not employ the response of a totalitarian government to the protests. In this context it was clear that segregation in restaurants, on transport and in other public 'accommodations' would not survive determined federal action. But that is not to say that it would be easy, as was shown on 15 September when bombers destroyed the 16th Street Baptist Church in Birmingham — headquarters of the protesters earlier in the year — killing four children. Two black youths were also killed in separate incidents the same day. Segregationists seemed determined to resist any attempts to force change, and blacks would still face intimidation and violence.

Voter registration and the 1964 Civil Rights Act

The final phase in the struggle to change the South was underway and once again the leaders of the civil rights movement were contemplating how to move the struggle forward and achieve their goals. It was clear that the movement needed to target the right to vote as the next key objective. Campaigners had forced desegregation in many public places in the South, and they could see that although change would not always be rapid, the tide had turned in favour of integrated restaurants, shops and transport. Nevertheless, blacks were still routinely denied the right to vote by a range of measures. 'Literacy' tests were designed to bamboozle potential voters, and a host of property qualifications and other regulations excluded blacks. Many were simply turned away on polling day. Until they could get the vote, they would not be able to achieve permanent change, as the state and federal government could continue to ignore them. The vote would also give them a permanent say in the nation's affairs. This was the final, but most important, hurdle.

Voter registration was a particular concern of the SNCC, which was committed to long-term projects to increase the black electorate. It was not easy to convince blacks to register: many were fearful of reprisals should they try to do so. The SNCC established a number of full-time paid workers in southern cities but they lacked resources. They also faced constant intimidation and violence — a number of activists were murdered in this period. The case of three civil rights workers killed in 1964 is perhaps the best known. Andrew Goodman, Michael Schwerner and James Chaney were murdered on 21 June near the town of Philadelphia in Mississippi. The subsequent FBI investigation moved slowly, and although arrests were made it was difficult to secure convictions. This was not an isolated incident, and the dangers of working for organisations such as CORE or SNCC in the South were very apparent to those involved. Medgar Evers, the NAACP's field officer in Mississippi, was assassinated on 12 June 1963. Byron De La Beckwith, a member of the Citizen's Council in the town of Greenwood, was charged with his murder but acquitted, and later ran as Democratic candidate for the post of lieutenant governor of the state.

It was clear that getting the blacks the vote was not going to be an easy task. In the meantime there was encouraging news for the civil rights movement. The Civil Rights Act initiated by Kennedy in the summer of 1963 was signed into law on 2 July 1964. After Kennedy's assassination on 22 November 1963, Vice-President Lyndon B. Johnson, a southerner from Texas, became president. Johnson used the national goodwill towards him, and also his own links with southern Democrats, to get the bill through Congress without substantial alteration. The Civil Rights Act of 1964 outlawed segregation in all public places such as restaurants and cinemas. It also gave the attorney general the power to prosecute any institutions that failed to integrate. It allowed the federal government to deny federal funds to any state that failed to act, and also set up the Equal Employment Opportunity Commission.

The 1964 Act was the most substantial and effective federal intervention on behalf of the blacks since the Fifteenth Amendment, and marked the success of the first phase of the campaign to secure African-Americans equality under the law. However, the Act left the issue of voting untouched. The various means by which blacks were denied any political say in the running of the South were still intact. The movement would have to bring pressure to bear on the federal government to legislate effectively on this issue. A number of approaches would be adopted. First, there were the long-running voter registration drives that had been underway since 1960 and were being coordinated by organisations such as the SNCC and later the Council of Federated Organizations (COFO). These had been quite successful in increasing the black electorate in the South, but were still a very gradual process. Second, activists from outside the South could be mobilised to come down in large numbers to help increase voter registration and draw media attention to the campaign, which was what they tried to do in the 'Freedom Summer' of 1964. Third, activists decided to establish a new party, the Mississippi Freedom Democratic Party (MFDP), to challenge the Democratic Party's monopoly in the state and to represent the party in the presidential primaries the same year. Finally, they could adopt mass direct action campaigns similar to the ones in Albany and Birmingham to draw the international press to the South and instigate public confrontations with state authorities. The various civil rights groups were again hoping to create a synergy that would force the issue of voting rights into the open and push the federal government to act.

Direct action 4: Freedom Summer

The focus of the civil rights activists' activities would be Mississippi, which was the most segregated state in the South. It was also one of the most economically backward and had suffered from the migration of both blacks and whites leaving the state for better prospects elsewhere. Between 1950 and 1960 more than 300,000 blacks had left Mississippi for elsewhere, as had 75% of white college graduates. Mississippi seemed to represent all the problems of the South at their worst — racism, backwardness and economic stagnation. The Civil Rights Act of 1964 had meant little to most blacks in the state, and there was a risk of the movement stagnating in the face of white opposition and black reluctance to face terrible danger. The SNCC's campaign was also beginning to run out of energy, and the winter of 1963–64 saw a wave of bombings, shootings and murder organised by the local Ku Klux Klan. In response to this the local SNCC leader Robert Moses proposed a mass action involving northern activists and southern civil rights workers aimed at drawing media attention to the region. He wanted over 1,000 white students to come to Mississippi and spend 2 months in the state working on voter registration. He stated:

> Previous projects have gotten little or no national publicity…and hence little national support either from public opinion or from the federal government. A large number of students from the North making the necessary sacrifices to go South would make it abundantly clear that this is not a situation which can be ignored any longer.

Moses' plan was radical but it promised to end the stalemate that seemed to have emerged in Mississippi in the previous 2 years. It was unpopular with some local SNCC workers who resented the fact that the whites would only be in the state for a short time but would be presented as 'saving' the movement from failure. Others were suspicious of any white involvement at all at this stage. Some SNCC workers were arming themselves in the face of Klan violence and encouraging local blacks to do the same. There were guns in the SNCC's Freedom House in Greenwood, and SNCC leaders such as Charles Cobb went out and about armed to protect themselves. However, although some in the SNCC were beginning to move in more radical directions, the organisation as a whole was still committed to securing federal support and media attention through non-violent direct action.

Some historians argue that there were other reasons for getting whites involved in Mississippi, and that the SNCC deliberately courted retaliation by white racists. If some northern whites were to be attacked by racist segregationists it would certainly generate publicity. A local SNCC member at the time, Ruby Doris Smith, stated: 'We know that the summer project was conceived with the idea of bloodshed.' The SNCC membership as a whole, though, probably supported the plan in the end because it offered some chance of ending the deadlock. As Moses stated: 'We needed an enormous amount of outside support to punch a hole in the segregationist system.' This support would be welcomed wherever it came from, and if it took northern whites to generate attention then that is what would happen.

Robert Kennedy, the attorney general, had been aware that the 'Freedom Summer' could well end in bloodshed from the moment it was conceived. President Johnson was warned that there could be deaths and that the local police force and the Klan were often one and the same organisation. The murder of Chaney, Schwerner and Goodman in the opening days of the campaign showed that the FBI would have to get involved at some level in trying to avert more bloodshed. Johnson pressured the director of the FBI, J. Edgar Hoover, to solve the case and infiltrate the Klan. He also sent the former head of the CIA, Allen Dulles, to Mississippi. Soon there were over 150 FBI agents in the state and it was clear that the federal government was serious in its intention to shut the Klan down in the state. But violence continued: in total over the summer of 1964 more than 1,000 people were arrested, 80 people were beaten and six people were murdered. In addition to this 35 churches were burned to the ground. It was no wonder that many in the SNCC despaired of a solution. The sheer level of violence had depressed many. The mayor of Jackson, Allen Thompson, had prepared for the summer protests by purchasing an armoured personnel carrier and recruiting an additional 100 police officers. He openly stated, 'They won't have a chance,' and promised, 'We are going to be ready for them.'

More than 800 white activists arrived in the state in waves from 21 June 1964. They registered blacks for the Mississippi Freedom Democratic Party (MFDP) and set up Freedom Schools across the state. Doctors offered free healthcare in Freedom Clinics and there were even Freedom Theatres set up to offer entertainment to locals. The aim was to galvanise the local black community and to focus the nation's attention on the state of race relations in the South. Johnson was worried by the emergence of the MFDP and its intention to send delegates to the Democratic Party convention that same year. These worries increased when the Californian Democratic primary recognised the MFDP rather than the local Democratic Party as the real representatives of Mississippi. Votes were now at stake and there was a real possibility that the presidential primaries could be disrupted by infighting among party members. The Republican candidate Barry Goldwater also threatened President Johnson's election chances.

Johnson saw his chances of keeping the presidency disappearing in bitter conflict after the Atlantic City convention. He decided to act. He arranged a compromise whereby two members of the MFDP would be allowed to the convention as delegates but would not represent Mississippi. All but three of the Mississippi delegates boycotted the convention in response to this deal, but Johnson had avoided splitting the party and had sidestepped an open confrontation at the convention. He had effectively destroyed the MFDP's chances of representing Mississippi at the convention, but the confrontation had made him determined to sort out the issue of voting rights once and for all. He told Nicholas Katzenbach, his new attorney general, to write 'the god-damnedest, toughest voting rights act you can devise'.

The Freedom Summer and the emergence of the MFDP had made plenty of headlines that summer. Once again the segregationists had been challenged to integrate and once again there had been violence. However, it was clear that time was running out for the whites who refused to integrate in the South. President Johnson was now determined to act to get blacks the vote, and he had had enough of certain southern states' refusal to integrate. In Mississippi, Freedom Summer had stirred up a lot of trouble but had also achieved some positive outcomes. The Johnson administration continued to fund some of the health clinics and schools set up by volunteers that summer. A national preschool enrichment programme known as Project Head Start evolved from the Freedom Summer programme in Mississippi. Black and white activists had worked together throughout the state. Many schools had been forced to integrate and there was no doubt that some blacks in Mississippi had benefited from newfound confidence in their struggle for equality.

However, the Freedom Summer had not been a total success. The failure of the MFDP to represent Mississippi and the compromise negotiated at the Atlantic City convention convinced some blacks that they had been betrayed. The failure of other white activists to stop the compromise convinced them that the whites would always try to hold them back. Many in the SNCC were disillusioned by the experience and this encouraged some to take a growing interest in the Black Power movement developing at the time. Robert Moses, who had engineered the Freedom Summer and come up with the idea of involving white activists in the movement to help focus attention on Mississippi, vowed not to have anything to do with the political system any more, and others were also disillusioned. Charles Sherrod, another SNCC activist, felt that the whole MFDP compromise showed that 'we are a country of racists'.

But despite some members of the SNCC losing faith in the political process, the Freedom Summer had won some important positive outcomes for the civil rights movement. National attention was once again focused on the issue. President Johnson was determined to push through a new voting rights Act and the MFDP had highlighted the lack of political opportunities offered to blacks in Mississippi. The fact that the SNCC had worked together with CORE, SCLC and other organisations was also important. In fact, as the Freedom Summer ended, Martin Luther King and the SCLC were already organising another campaign to continue the momentum built up over the summer. They planned to return to Alabama and again try to effect change through non-violent direct action.

This time they chose the town of Selma as the focal point for the campaign. Selma contained more than 15,000 black people of voting age, of whom only 335 had managed to register. The town epitomised the central problem of the civil rights movement: getting the vote. It also employed a battery of regulations to try to exclude blacks from the vote. Complex application forms, certificates of 'good character', proofs of residency and identification all blocked blacks from registering. Most effective, however, were the 'constitutional interpretation tests' that were demanded by electoral registrars. These tests consisted of complex questions that often had no clear answer and were designed to confuse potential voters: blacks were failed, while whites passed.

Direct action 5:
the Selma–Montgomery March

Selma had a particularly active Citizens' Council and an openly racist and violent sheriff, Jim Clark. The state judge was James A. Hare, a notorious segregationist. The governor of Alabama was George Corley Wallace, who had already stirred up violence with his vow to maintain 'segregation forever'. Conditions were ideal for confrontation and the SCLC was determined to ensure that once again the violent injustice of the system was exposed for the world to see. Selma also had a strong local movement, the Dallas County Voters' League, led by Rev. Frederick D. Reese and Mrs Amelia P. Boynton. This group had asked for the SCLC's help and was determined to succeed. SCLC activist Ralph Abernathy recalled: 'With any luck we would be visibly abused without being maimed or killed. The line we walked was increasingly thin in these matters.'

The SCLC was prepared to widen the confrontation by protesting in neighbouring counties. Martin Luther King was clear: 'In a crisis we must have a sense of drama.' In fact, the SCLC did not need to worry that Jim Clark would respond subtly to their challenges — he arrested more than 3,500 blacks and was happy to beat and intimidate protesters in full view of the media. However, the world's media needed more to sustain their attention. King decided to embark on 'broader forms of civil disobedience'. On 18 February 1965 Sheriff Clark and his state troopers had attacked a night march in the town of Marion. One of the troopers had shot a young black man, Jimmie Lee Jackson. Jackson had taken 8 days to die, and during this time King decided to force a showdown with Governor Wallace by proposing a 54-mile march from Selma to Montgomery. Wallace was based in Montgomery and King hoped to place the blame for Jimmie Lee Jackson's death on him. Albert Turner, a local activist from Marion, recalled:

> We was infuriated to the point where we wanted to carry Jimmy's body to George Wallace and dump it on the steps of the Capitol. We had decided we were going to get killed or we was going to be free.

The march was planned for Sunday 7 March 1965. Governor George Wallace announced that it would be halted by his state troopers, and even the SNCC asked the SCLC to put off the march and avoid escalating a tense situation. John Lewis wrote to King that 'the objectives of the march do not justify the dangers'. King was determined to push ahead. He met President Johnson on 5 February to discuss the proposed voting rights bill. He was convinced that continued pressure was needed to make the president push through a bill that would really guarantee blacks the vote, and that the protests should continue.

The march took place on 7 March as planned. Martin Luther King was not present, so SCLC leader Hosea Williams led it: more than 600 marchers set off. When they arrived at the nearby Edmund Pettus Bridge they were halted by Alabama state troopers, many of them on horseback, who attacked the demonstrators and fired tear gas. The violence was shocking, and the media transmitted images of it across America. Mayor Smitherman later recalled that the scenes 'looked like war' and that they brought down the 'wrath of the nation' on the town authorities. Condemnation of the police action was universal; even some white southerners condemned it. An aide wrote to Johnson that the public felt 'the deepest sense of outrage it has ever felt on the civil rights question'. There were protests outside the White House and at the Justice Department, and marches across America: in New York, Detroit, Chicago, Boston and Los Angeles. More than 400 ministers, nuns and clergy went to Selma immediately to support the marchers. The civil rights movement finally had its own 'Bloody

Sunday' to rouse the righteous indignation of public opinion. It was clear that a critical moment had occurred — *Time* labelled it 'an orgy of police brutality'.

Public opinion was now swinging firmly behind Martin Luther King and the SCLC. King was quick to act, stating, 'No American is without responsibility' and confirming that he would lead another march to Montgomery on Tuesday 9 March. The stage was set for a further vicious confrontation, particularly as Governor Wallace vowed, 'We can't give one inch. We're going to enforce state law.' The SCLC appealed to district court judge Frank M. Thompson to support their right to march, but Thompson said that he would make a decision on Thursday. As at Albany, the leaders of the civil rights movement had to decide whether to act without the support of the federal government. This time they decided that the march would go ahead. King vowed that he would 'rather die on the highway in Alabama than make a butchery of conscience by compromising with evil'. In fact, the march was something of a disappointment, as King only led the marchers to the police line at Pettus Bridge and then retreated. He was accused of having made a secret deal with the federal government, but he argued that to provoke more violence was pointless. He believed that 'having made our point, revealing the continued presence of violence and showing clearly who were the oppressed and who were the oppressors', a tactical retreat was justified.

King did stay in Selma, however, and urged others to do so. One of them, white Unitarian minister James Reeb, was murdered that night by a gang of white men. This event inflamed public opinion even more and led Judge Johnson to make a public statement that the 'federal government is engaged in preparing legislation which will secure the right to vote for every American'. On 13 March George Wallace met with President Johnson in Washington. Johnson appealed to the governor's sense of history and urged him to support the civil rights movement in his state. The following evening, on 14 March, the president made a televised statement to Congress in support of the voting rights legislation. He urged them to support the bill and used the language of the movement itself in his summing up statement, promising, 'We shall overcome.'

Civil rights leaders in Selma were alternately buoyed up by Johnson's statement and depressed by continued police violence. On 14 March SNCC chairman James Forman led a march to the Capitol building in Montgomery to support the call for voting rights and again the marchers were badly beaten by police. Calls for a march continued, and when the federal judge supported their right to do so the way was cleared for the march to take place on Sunday 21 March. President Johnson had federalised the Alabama National Guard and ordered them to protect the march. He also sent in 2,000 soldiers and 100 FBI agents, and a further 100 federal marshals were protecting the marchers. George

Wallace was not going to be allowed to stop it. That Sunday more than 4,000 people met to join the march. The distance was 54 miles. King led the march and it was supported from a headquarters in Selma. Food and tents were shuttled out to the marchers, and by the final day numbers had grown to over 25,000. A plot to assassinate King failed to materialise and the marchers entered Montgomery 4 days later. King was joined by other notable figures in the movement, including Rosa Parks, Philip Randolph and John Lewis. There was a sense both of history and of success that day. King stated that the 'arc of the universe is long, but it bends towards justice'.

Voting Rights Act

As the march ended there was a sense that the tide had turned in favour of the civil rights movement in the South. The president had once again intervened decisively to support a public protest, the federal judges had ruled in favour of the protesters and violence had failed to stop blacks marching for freedom. However, the murder of Viola Liuzzo, a white woman from Detroit helping to ferry black marchers back to Selma at the end of the march, showed that the Klan were still prepared to kill in a bid to stop integration. The violence and murders that had taken place during the Selma campaign demonstrated that there were many in the South who would resist the civil rights movement, but it was also clear that such actions would now fail to stop it. The passing of the Voting Rights Act further reinforced this 5 months later. It made literacy tests, 'constitutional interpretation tests' and 'good character' requirements illegal. It covered Louisiana, Mississippi, Alabama, Georgia, South Carolina, North Carolina and Virginia. It also gave the federal government power to intervene if the Act was not enforced.

The Voting Rights Act finally gave the blacks the vote and enforced the provisions of the Fifteenth Amendment passed in 1870. It had taken almost a century to ensure that African-Americans were guaranteed the rights that they had first won after the Civil War. The Act marked the defeat of the segregationists and the end of the overt system of racism that had denied the blacks equal opportunity in the South. It also marked the high point of Martin Luther King's influence and the success of the policy of non-violence.

The achievements of the civil rights movement between 1954 and 1965 were enormous. Blacks had ended more than 300 years of state-sponsored oppression and become participants in civil society in the South. The racism and violence of the segregationists had been challenged, and the federal government had intervened decisively to enforce equality and the rule of law. The leadership of Martin Luther King and other black leaders had generated the respect and admiration of Americans throughout the land. A new class of black politicians and civic leaders emerged in the years after the Voting Rights Act, and a new generation of blacks voted for them.

However, after a decade of success the civil rights movement would enter a new phase of division and more complex challenges. Lack of equal economic and housing opportunities, the more covert racism of the North and the problems of avoiding a violent response to these issues would occupy the attention of black community leaders after 1965. The movement would fragment: new leaders would emerge and new tactics would be adopted by blacks still struggling to secure the same opportunities as whites.

Questions

1 'Civil rights activists forced the federal government to end segregation in the South.' Do you agree with this viewpoint?

2 Was 'direct action' the most effective tactic for challenging segregation in the South?

3 'The Voting Rights Act was inevitable by 1965.' Discuss.

How successful was the civil rights movement?

At the start of this book it was suggested that the election of Barack Obama as president signified that the civil rights movement had achieved its goals. Today, segregation is illegal and blacks can vote. There are many black officials in the South. The armed forces are integrated. Black officials helped head President Bush's government. Yet as was also indicated at the start of the book, there is still massive economic inequality. There is still a sense that real equality remains a distant goal. Alabama state representative Alvin Holmes stated:

> Progress has been made, but we're still fighting for equality. Racism and segregation is no longer de jure but it is still de facto. Whites still don't want to live near blacks. The schools are resegregating because housing is still segregated. The fight's not over.

While optimists might point to Obama, others point to New Orleans as the real face of race relations in America. An entire city appeared to be abandoned by the federal government during the Hurricane Katrina crisis in 2005, with some suggesting this was because it was mainly inhabited by poor blacks. Many problems surrounding race relations in American have not been resolved, and there is much contradictory experience to be examined.

Gary Younge highlighted this problem when he wrote: 'For many white Americans the passage of civil rights legislation…drew a line under the civil rights era. Since there were now no legal barriers to black participation, some chose to ignore the economic, social and political barriers that remained.' These barriers have actually proved harder to shift, as they are so much more entrenched and less tangible. The immediate aftermath of the Voting Rights Act was probably the high point of the civil rights movement. There was a sense of well-earned satisfaction that justice had finally been done and that blacks could now begin to close the gaps with whites. Yet this was very short-lived. Congress passed the Voting Rights Act in July 1965, and in August the Watts district of Los Angeles erupted into race rioting that killed 34 people and left thousands injured and arrested. The campaign in the South had not solved problems in the North; in fact, events over the following decades were to show that economic inequality and deprivation would be as hard to overcome as overt legal discrimination. In some ways it would be harder, as there was no clear target to focus on — the goals were much more amorphous and intangible. Maintaining the momentum of the struggle in such circumstances would not be easy.

Black radicalism

The Watts riots of 11–15 August 1965 arose out of tensions between local black young people and the police. They were sparked by the arrest of a black youth, Marquette Frye. Hundreds of businesses and homes were burnt, millions of dollars' worth of damage was caused, and the National Guard was called in to restore order. Eventually an uneasy calm returned. Investigations into the riots highlighted poor housing, unemployment and lack of education as some of the factors leading up to the explosion of violence.

Almost three decades later, in 1992, riots again broke out in the city. This time they were even worse than in 1965 and were televised worldwide. The trigger once again was police tensions with the local community, following the acquittal of four police officers filmed attacking a black suspect, Rodney King. Some 53 people were killed in these riots, and there was widespread looting and arson. The causes of the riots were again more complex than the initial trigger event, and the violence highlighted the differing social and economic conditions faced by blacks and whites. It seemed to many onlookers that three decades had led to little real change and that the civil rights movement had failed to capitalise on the promise of the Voting Rights Act. Blacks were still poor, still out of work and still excluded from the American Dream. The violence surrounding the flooding of New Orleans in August 2005 as Hurricane Katrina broke the city's defensive levées seemed to confirm the view that for blacks in America, 'nothing really changes'.

Is this viewpoint justified? Black radicals in the latter part of the 1960s argued that it was. After the Voting Rights Act the civil rights movement splintered into factions. The SNCC had flirted with Black Nationalism for some time, frustrated by the slow pace of change and white violence in the Freedom Summer. Stokely Carmichael, one of the SNCC's leaders, had become disillusioned with peaceful protest as an effective agent for change. Other prominent leaders in the black community had also argued that it was time for black people to stand up and fight. Malcolm X, possibly the best known of these figures, openly contrasted his stance with that of Martin Luther King. He had stated that non-violence was the 'philosophy of the fool' and in response to Rev. King's famous 'I have a dream' speech he had said: 'While King was having a dream, the rest of us Negroes are having a nightmare.' Malcolm X toned down some of his inflammatory rhetoric in the period before his assassination, but he achieved notoriety by arguing that black people had a right to defend themselves against white racists. In 1965 he said: 'Be peaceful, be courteous, obey the law, respect everyone; but if someone puts his hand on you, send him to the cemetery.' He had voiced the thoughts of many of his fellow African-Americans when he argued that 'turning the other cheek' was not always the right path. He believed that it was when people got angry that they brought about change and that it was time that the blacks got angry enough to force change if need be.

Malcolm X had joined the Nation of Islam in the 1950s. This small and eccentric organisation had some strange (and some would argue sinister) beliefs, but it offered small-time criminal Malcolm Little a way out of crime and a means of regaining his self-respect. He joined the organisation when it numbered in the hundreds, and his oratory and contribution helped it to grow in popularity in the 1950s under the leadership of Elijah Muhammad to over 25,000 members by 1963. Malcolm Little became Malcolm X (a common practice, as many in the Nation of Islam argued that surnames were 'slave' names). The Nation of Islam and Malcolm X attracted growing attention from the black community, and they worried white law enforcement organisations. The FBI had been monitoring Rev. Martin Luther King for years, convinced he was a Communist, but it was even more concerned by Malcolm X. He became a well-known international figure and travelled widely in Africa and Europe. He made the pilgrimage to Mecca and saw his role as helping to liberate African-Americans from their servitude. Rivals from the Nation of Islam assassinated him after he left it. Although he has been remembered as a radical proponent of Black Nationalism and linked to calls for violence against whites, there is plenty of evidence that he was moderating his views as he matured. In a speech made before his death entitled 'The ballot or the bullet', he urged blacks to use their right to vote wisely. Malcolm X inspired many to be more decisive in fighting for their rights. Such people believed that Martin Luther King was too moderate and 'gradualist'.

With the passing of the Voting Rights Act attention turned to economic inequality and also to the North. Martin Luther King tried to mobilise popular protests against segregated housing and lack of economic opportunity in the northern cities such as Chicago. He also publicly opposed the war in Vietnam, angering President Johnson, who felt betrayed by King's opposition to the conflict. In 1968 King and the SCLC organised the Poor People's Campaign, which attempted to focus attention on continuing economic divisions between the black and white communities and culminated in a march on Washington that was badly attended. Individuals and groups within the civil rights movement were by now openly bickering about the future of the movement and there was a definite sense that momentum was being lost. In fact, it was while supporting a trade union strike in Memphis, Tennessee, that King was assassinated. On 3 April 1968 he had spoken to a large congregation at the church of Mason Temple and given one of his most memorable speeches. He had acknowledged that he faced threats, saying:

> Then I got into Memphis. And some began to say the threats, or talk about the threats that were out. What would happen to me from some of our sick white brothers? Well, I don't know what will happen now. We've got some difficult days ahead.

But he also showed the faith that had supported him in the long years of struggle when he continued:

> But it doesn't matter with me now, because I've been to the mountaintop. And I don't mind. Like anybody, I would like to live a long life. Longevity has its place. But I'm not concerned about that now. I just want to do God's will. And He's allowed me to go up to the mountain. And I've looked over. And I've seen the promised land. I may not get there with you. But I want you to know tonight, that we, as a people, will get to the promised land. And so I'm happy, tonight. I'm not worried about anything. I'm not fearing any man. Mine eyes have seen the glory of the coming of the Lord.

It was his last speech. The following evening he was assassinated in the Lorraine Motel by James Earl Ray, a white racist. There were various allegations of a conspiracy but these were never proven. The assassination sparked a wave of violent riots across America in more than 100 cities. It seemed to confirm the view of radical blacks who had argued that the establishment would always react with violence to African-Americans' attempts to achieve equality. The riots in the aftermath of King's assassination followed a familiar pattern, as black youths fought with police and destroyed much of the infrastructure of their local communities. After the riots it took over 2 months to catch King's killer.

Following King's death the civil rights movement never again achieved the cohesion that it had enjoyed in the 1950s and early 1960s. There would be marches and protests, and various leaders would attempt to lead the struggle, but America was entering a new phase of race relations and times had changed. Black Nationalism was one of many strands of the civil rights movement that survived the 1960s, but it was too vague and divisive to rally the community around it. Many black commentators criticise Black Nationalism and argue that in reality it is as bigoted and intolerant as white racism. However, actions such as the Black Power salutes given at the 1968 Olympics by Tommie Smith and

John Carlos attracted widespread attention from the world media and maintained some focus on the issue of black rights in America.

The Black Nationalism and Black Power movements that emerged in the late 1960s were diverse and vague in their ambitions. Many of the people involved in them openly embraced violence, while some even began to stray into criminality, becoming involved in drug smuggling and shoot-outs with the police. The most infamous group to emerge from the Black Power movement is the Black Panther Party, which appeared in Oakland, California. Its stated aim was to protect the black community by harassing racist police forces and carrying out various acts of social agitation. It was founded in October 1966 by Huey Newton and Bobby Seale and it spread across America. By 1968 it had 5,000 members and its newspaper, the *Black Panther*, was selling over 250,000 copies. However, it was increasingly difficult to say what it stood for. Some heavily armed members followed police patrols and harassed them. Others set up community centres and tried to encourage local projects aimed at increasing employment and opportunities in the black community. There was a brief merger with the SNCC, but both organisations were beginning to fall apart. The trial of one of the Black Panther leaders, Huey Newton, led to his conviction, and a number of gun battles with the police cut the leadership down further, with many Panthers killed or imprisoned. By the mid-1970s the Black Panther Party had collapsed, although it continued to exert a cultural influence on many people who found its 'radical chic' glamorous.

Affirmative action

Black Nationalism seemed to peak in the late 1960s, and by the 1970s it was in decline. Various other radical groups appeared and disappeared in bewildering succession; some espoused violence, while others were radical but largely peaceful. The SNCC disintegrated in the 1970s. Groups such as the Black Liberation Army and the Black Panthers occasionally linked to other 'New Left' groups but after the end of the Vietnam War in 1973 the political climate became more settled. The civil rights struggle continued, but it became more diverse as a range of groups focused on different areas. Other groups also competed for attention: women, gays and Hispanic groups were some of those who argued for increased political and economic power. The picture for African-Americans also became more blurred: in the South, growing numbers achieved political office, and affirmative action programmes became increasingly common.

The idea of helping blacks to achieve equality was not a new one. At the end of the Civil War General Sherman had promised 'respectable negroes' 40 acres and a mule, and the Freedman's Bureau was set up to help blacks in the South, although its work was largely reversed by segregationists after the failure of reconstruction. President Kennedy first used the term 'affirmative action' in 1961, when his Executive Order 10925 urged federal government contractors to employ African-Americans. Although blacks had achieved equality before the law in 1964 and 1965, it was still difficult for them to break through what they perceived as a 'colour bar' that stopped them getting into college and professions such as medicine and the law.

In the late 1960s some states had introduced bussing programmes to get black children into predominantly white schools, and universities had also adopted affirmative action programmes. School bussing programmes aroused widespread protests. In the 1971 *Swann* v *Charlotte-Mecklenburg Board of Education* ruling, the Supreme Court allowed the federal government to force mandatory bussing on Charlotte, North Carolina, and other cities nationwide in an attempt to encourage greater integration. This was limited in 1974 when the Supreme Court ruled that students could only be bussed across district lines when evidence of segregation across multiple school districts existed. President Nixon proved reluctant to support bussing and stated in 1971: 'I have consistently opposed the bussing of our nation's schoolchildren to achieve a racial balance, and I am opposed to the bussing of children simply for the sake of bussing.' In Boston in 1974 there were attacks on buses carrying black children to white schools, and a protest group called ROAR (Restore Our Alienated Rights) formed to combat attempts to integrate schools in this way. In turn the black community in Boston organised actions in support of bussing: the result was a qualified success, as a local judge took the school system out of the control of the school committee to try to force it to segregate.

The passions aroused in Boston demonstrated the problems encountered by the black community in America after 1965. They still faced overt discrimination and would have to struggle for their rights to be respected. President Johnson recognised this in 1965, in a speech at Howard University, a black university in Washington, DC. He said:

> You do not take a person who for years has been hobbled by chains and liberate him, bring him up to the starting line of a race and then say, 'You are free to complete with all the others,' and still justly believe that you have been completely fair.

The implication of this was that affirmative action would be supported by the federal government. However, as the university and bussing controversies showed, positive discrimination would still be resisted. In time the bussing issue became less contentious, but not necessarily for the right reasons. By the 1980s, desegregation bussing declined as whites moved to suburbs far away from city centres and so made it impractical. Many black families opposed the idea of subjecting their children to long bus journeys to distant schools simply for the sake of integration. By the 1990s most school districts had been released from court supervision and ceased using mandatory bussing to try to desegregate schools.

It remains an issue, but in recent years attention has shifted to quota systems, which although difficult to implement have been judged necessary on occasion. For example, in 1970 the Alabama Police Department was taken to court over its hiring policies and the fact that no black police officers had ever been employed. In 1987 it was back in court, accused of failing to promote black police officers beyond entry level, and strict quotas were ordered to combat the overt racism of the force. Similar quotas have been adopted by other institutions with varying degrees of success, but they remain complicated to implement and difficult to enforce. They have also been challenged by groups that oppose the idea of quotas perceived as favouring one group over another. Supporters of affirmative action programmes argue that they are necessary and have led to increased numbers of blacks attending university, helping a confident and wealthy black middle class to emerge. Yet positive discrimination remains controversial, and whites denied entry to certain universities have challenged the system.

The most significant challenge came in 1978, in what became known as the *Bakke* decision. Allan Bakke, a white student, was twice refused admission by the medical school of the University of California, which retained 16% of its places for ethnic minority students. Bakke sued the university, claiming that others had been admitted to the university despite having lower grades. Accusing the university of 'reverse discrimination', he insisted that his civil rights had been violated and that this breached both the Fourteenth Amendment to the Constitution and the 1964 Civil Rights Act. The US Supreme Court, in a far from unanimous decision, upheld Bakke's claims and ordered the university to admit him. It ruled that affirmative action was constitutional but that strict racial quotas should be avoided. Following the decision, several states abandoned affirmative action programmes altogether and almost all abandoned quotas based on racial or ethnic origin.

In the 2003 *Gratz* v *Bollinger* case two white plaintiffs (Jennifer Gratz and Patrick Hamacher) appealed against the University of Michigan's affirmative action admissions policy and received partial support from the Supreme Court. The University of Michigan was forced to modify its points-based entry system but was still allowed to factor race into its calculations. In June 2007 two court cases challenged affirmative action. In *Parents Involved in Community Schools* v *Seattle School District No. 1* and *Meredith* v *Jefferson County Board of Education*, the Supreme Court ruled that programmes in Seattle and in Louisville, Kentucky, which tried to maintain diversity in schools by considering race when assigning students to schools were unconstitutional. In November 2008 Nebraska voted to ban affirmative action altogether.

The end of the movement?

Despite these challenges, affirmative action programmes still survive and continue to offer opportunities that arguably would otherwise be denied to African-Americans. Yet the picture has become increasingly complex and some would contend, as did many commentators in the 2008 presidential election, that a 'post-racial' America is emerging. The 'colour bar' that seemed to exclude African-Americans from high office is no longer in evidence, with figures such as Colin Powell and Condoleezza Rice having occupied senior government posts. There are also many examples of mainstream black musicians and entertainers who have achieved huge success and remain fairly apolitical. While the rap band Public Enemy and musician Gil Scott Heron still embody the politics of protest in their work, others such as Sean Coombs (Puff Daddy or P. Diddy) seem content to make as much money as possible marketing their brands of music, clothing and entertainment.

Indeed the success of some black leaders has led to them being accused of 'selling out'. Harry Belafonte, the singer and civil rights activist, compared Colin Powell (Chairman of the Joint Chiefs of Staff) with a 'house slave'. The radical magazine *In These Times* accused Powell and Rice of serving in an 'Uncle Tom's cabinet', implying that entering high office represented a betrayal of their race. The Council on Black Internal Affairs set up after the Million Man March in 1995 published a derogatory *American Directory of Certified Uncle Toms* in 2002, which ranked over 50 black leaders on an 'Uncle Tom' rating and accused those listed of effectively 'selling out' their own black people. Colin Powell, Oprah Winfrey and Maya Angelou were all named. Such condemnation of successful African-Americans by other African-Americans is controversial, but in the 1950s there would not have been a list of 50 successful blacks to criticise. The fact that the black community is able to engage in such debates is, for some, an indication of how much it has moved on from the racial politics of the civil rights era.

Today, startling inequalities between black Americans and whites remain, with continuing poverty and disadvantage, seen for example in the problems of poor housing and high rates of unemployment and crime. Yet there are many success stories: for example, dozens of Congressmen and women are African-American. In October 2008 there were 641 African-American mayors in the USA. The large sums of money that black middle-class people donated to Barack Obama during his 2008 election campaign showed how much money and influence they can generate.

Recent successful prosecutions of individuals involved in some of the most notorious crimes of the civil rights period have also shown that times have changed. Since 1989, 23 murders have been re-examined in the South, resulting in 27 arrests and 22 convictions. In 1994, Byron De La Beckwith was eventually convicted of the 1963 murder of Medgar Evers and sentenced to life imprisonment. He died in 2001, still in prison. In 2005 Edgar Ray Killen was tried for the killings of the activists Chaney, Goodman and Schwerner in 1964, and sentenced to 60 years in prison. The fact that the states concerned have finally prosecuted such high-profile cases has shown that there is a willingness to try to confront old crimes and draw a line under the illegal activities of the past.

However, the fact that inequality is still so evident in such states worries some commentators. Professor Charles Payne of Duke University has argued that the South's desire to 'rebrand' itself and assert that 'the past is the past' reflects an attempt to deny that racial inequality still exists. Gary Younge summarised the central problem still facing African-Americans when he stated: 'Integration had won African-Americans the opportunity to eat in any restaurant. Only equality could ensure that they would be able to pay the bill.' Achieving that equality would prove much harder than anticipated. Economic and educational disadvantages would continue to hinder African-Americans' progress, while racism remained, albeit in a more discreet guise than before. For this reason some blacks in the South today would even argue that in some ways the situation was better under segregation: the system was clear, the racism undisguised. Ernest Brown, head of the NAACP in Rock Hill, South Carolina, observed in 1999:

When segregation went, we lost the very foundation of our community. You need your own [people]. When I was at school, the teachers had attitude and commitment. I don't see that towards our children now. We don't have any black teachers, administrators, coaches, class presidents, and valedictorians. When I was growing up no one said you couldn't achieve. I felt fortunate that I went to a black school. I joined the drama society, the choir and was always encouraged to be the best I could be. The equal is the only part I want…If we had the same facilities as the whites I don't care if we never went to school with them. I want the same buildings and the same kind of resources. I'm not bothered about sitting side by side with them.

The end of segregation meant the best black students went to white schools and colleges. Desegregation opened up the community to competition from the stronger and better-resourced white business and education sector. Evidence for this point of view can be seen in the success of the black colleges that still thrive in the South. There are 103 historically black colleges surviving from an era when it was impossible for blacks to attend white universities. Many have now opened their doors to white students in a strange reversal of fortunes. Their achievements are impressive and historically their role has been to provide a platform for the black middle class to secure successful careers. In the USA 85% of black doctors and 75% of black military officers have come from such colleges. The issue of segregation is still complex: in some cases the black community is choosing to remain segregated so as to improve its chances of success.

It is not easy to sum up the civil rights movement. When Barack Obama made his acceptance speech on 5 November 2008, marking the election of the USA's first African-American president, he chose to reflect on the civil rights movement and a century of change in America:

> This election had many firsts and many stories that will be told for generations. But one that's on my mind tonight is about a woman who cast her ballot in Atlanta. She's a lot like the millions of others who stood in line to make their voice heard in this election except for one thing — Ann Nixon Cooper is 106 years old. She was born just a generation past slavery; a time when there were no cars on the road or planes in the sky; when someone like her couldn't vote for two reasons — because she was a woman and because of the colour of her skin. And tonight, I think about all that she's seen throughout her century in America — the heartache and the hope; the struggle and the progress; the times we were told that we can't, and the people who pressed on with that American creed: Yes we can. At a time when women's voices were silenced and their hopes dismissed, she lived to see them stand up and speak out and reach for the ballot. Yes we can. When there was despair in the dust bowl and depression across the land, she saw a nation conquer fear itself with a New Deal, new jobs and a new sense of common purpose. Yes we can. When the bombs fell on our harbour and tyranny threatened the world, she was there to witness a generation rise to greatness and a democracy was saved. Yes we can. She was there for the buses in Montgomery, the hoses in Birmingham, a bridge in Selma, and a preacher from Atlanta who told a people that 'we shall overcome'. Yes we can.

Others are less positive about the prospects for blacks in the USA. They believe that the civil rights struggle in the 1950s and 1960s failed to solve the deep-rooted problems faced by the black community. Oliver Hill, one of the NAACP's principal lawyers in the 1950s, said in 1999:

> Nowadays we are dealing with the same issues. The white man still doesn't want to accept Negroes as fully fledged citizens...We were the ones who put up a big fight but everybody else moves faster than us. White women have benefited more than Negroes from the Civil Rights Acts of 1964 and 1965.

There is undoubtedly still discrimination, and many blacks remain disadvantaged. Yet there is also a feeling that times have moved on and that old racial divisions are no longer as substantial as they were. In modern-day America it is possible to be black and successful, and there is a substantial well-educated middle class of black people who feel they can achieve whatever they want. Yet there remain deep-rooted, long-term racial divisions that still decide many citizens' future prospects.

Questions

1 To what extent did American presidents help the civil rights movement between 1865 and 1965?
2 What was the major turning point for African-American civil rights in the period 1865–1965?
3 'African-Americans today face more significant social and economic barriers than political ones.' Do you agree with this viewpoint?

Photographs from the civil rights period

There is a huge amount of media resources on the civil rights movement. The further back you go, of course, the less material there is, and the black community in the South before the 1950s was traditionally neglected, but in the twentieth century the USA had a thriving media industry. The First Amendment guaranteed freedom of speech and of the press, so the media were always diverse. For this reason, looking at images of the civil rights movement is very different to looking at images from totalitarian regimes. The messages within the media images will not necessarily be as overt or propagandist, but you need to be aware that the presentation of information can still be one-sided and that there is as much 'spin' within the civil rights movement as in any other modern political process. Nevertheless, you will be able to find images that represent the South and the civil rights movement from all viewpoints.

There are some particularly iconic photographs that tend to define the period. Images of black children being bowled over by water sprayed from fire-hoses directed by 'Bull' Connor's police force in Birmingham, or Martin Luther King addressing the crowds in front of the Lincoln Memorial during the March on Washington, are replayed time and time again. The civil rights movement also attracted the attention of the whole world — it was a dramatic and inspiring story that was readily accessible. The struggle for equality taking place in the South was beamed across the globe, the Cold War context only serving to give it added significance. Here was the superpower that positioned itself as the worldwide defender of freedom denying its own citizens the rights it demanded other regimes grant their own people. Unsurprisingly, the propagandists of the Soviet Union used the civil rights movement to support their critique of America. They argued that the plight of the blacks highlighted the hypocrisy of the USA and the capitalist system that was responsible for such inequality. Even close allies of the USA found it difficult to understand how racial inequality could be allowed to continue, when the world had only recently defeated fascist regimes dedicated to upholding racial ideas not so far removed from those of the segregated South.

It is difficult to select two images that highlight the complexity of the civil rights movement. Broadly speaking, however, it is possible to divide the photographs of this period into two categories: those that portray the inequality and racism the blacks faced and those that show them fighting that inequality and racism. We shall therefore consider one of each.

Lynching

This grotesque image of a lynching is well known (in fact one could justly describe it as infamous) and often illustrates the pages of civil rights books. There are many images of lynchings in America but there is no denying the power of this one. In a way the bizarre thing about this picture is not the blacks who have been hanged without trial but the crowd that has gathered to witness the event. There is not the slightest sign of shame or revulsion. In fact, one could almost describe the atmosphere as festive.

There are a couple of other interesting facts about this picture. This lynching actually occurred in a town called Marion in Indiana, which is not in the South. This demonstrates that such actions occurred in states not usually associated with segregation. It also occurred in 1930 — a time when most people assume that such events were on the decline. It is the last recorded lynching in the northern USA. The two men hung that day (Thomas Shripp and Abram Smith) were accused of killing a store owner and raping his girlfriend. The fact that

lynching remained a feature of justice in America up until the 1930s shows how acceptable some people felt that this form of 'frontier justice' was.

'I have a dream'

This photo of Martin Luther King was taken while he was giving his 'I have a dream' speech at the March on Washington demonstration on 28 August 1963. President Kennedy, fearing widespread unrest, had pleaded with the civil rights leaders planning the march to call it off, but in fact the day passed peacefully. A quarter of a million people turned up for the march, and King was the final speaker.

His speech is remembered most clearly for its closing passage in which he envisaged the day when 'the sons of former slaves and the sons of former slave owners will be able to sit down together at the table of brotherhood'. The finale of the speech was unexpected: he was about to finish when Mahalia Jackson (a famous singer standing nearby) urged him to go on. He then continued, using a speech he had given a week earlier in Detroit. His dream of a society where race was no longer a barrier to opportunity has continued to inspire the movement and has stamped King clearly in the collective identity. It was a defining moment in the civil rights movement. Some activists at the time felt that the focus on Martin Luther King was unfair and obscured some of the issues they were fighting for. However, the nature of the modern media made it likely that some kind of iconic figure would be sought and King fulfilled that role.

Martin Luther King remains the face of the civil rights movement in this era. He is still the most recognisable of the movement's leaders and has become an internationally respected figure. In 1964 he received the Nobel Peace Prize, and his assassination in 1968 was widely seen as one of the tragedies of the age. The importance of his leadership is marked in the USA by Martin Luther King Day, the third Monday in January (around the time of King's birthday). One of only three federal holidays to commemorate an individual (the other two celebrate George Washington, the first American president, and Christopher Columbus, who is credited with discovering the continent in 1492), it was signed into law by Ronald Reagan in 1983 and observed for the first time in 1986. However, some states resisted holding it or combined it with other holidays. It was officially observed in all 50 states for the first time in 2000. The King Center in Atlanta, Georgia, is dedicated to continuing his work, and various museums commemorate his life and achievements.

Timeline

1787 US Constitution signed

1861–65 American Civil War ends slavery in the USA

1866–77 Reconstruction: Congress attempts to end segregation in the South

1896 *Plessy* v *Ferguson* supports segregation with 'separate but equal' principle

1909 National Association for the Advancement of Colored People (NAACP) founded

1919–22 Rise and fall of the United Negro Improvement Association (UNIA) under Marcus Garvey

1942 Congress of Racial Equality (CORE) founded

1946 President's Committee on Civil Rights set up by Truman

1947 Truman addresses annual meeting of the NAACP

1948 Segregation ended in the armed forces

1954 *Brown* v *Board of Education, Topeka* rules segregation in education is unconstitutional

1955 Murder of Emmett Till leads to international focus on lynching and white violence

1955–56 Montgomery bus boycott

1956 Supreme Court deems transport segregation 'unconstitutional'

1957 Southern Christian Leadership Conference (SCLC) founded, with Martin Luther King as president

Little Rock crisis, Arkansas

1960 Sit-ins started in Greensboro, North Carolina; Student Nonviolent Coordinating Committee (SNCC) set up

1961 Freedom rides started

1961–62 Albany campaign attempts to mobilise a whole community against segregation

1962 Riots at Mississippi State University as James Meredith (first black student) attends: two people killed and dozens injured

1963 **April–May:** Birmingham, Alabama, campaign

   12 June: Medgar Evers, civil rights leader in Mississippi, murdered

   28 August: March on Washington; Martin Luther King's 'I have a dream' speech

   22 November: President John F. Kennedy assassinated; succeeded by Lyndon B. Johnson as 36th president

1964 Civil Rights Act and Martin Luther King receives Nobel Peace Prize

1965 Selma campaigns and the march to Montgomery; Voting Rights Act

   11–15 August: riots in Watts area of Los Angeles: dozens killed and large areas of the city destroyed

1968 **4 April:** Martin Luther King assassinated in Memphis, Tennessee; riots erupted in over 100 cities in the USA

1970 Daniel Patrick Moynihan, adviser to President Richard M. Nixon, urges racial matters need a period of 'benign neglect'

1978 Supreme Court's *Bakke* decision confirms constitutionality of affirmative action programmes but rules against observing strict racial quotas

1984 Jesse Jackson unsuccessful in attempt to win Democratic Party presidential nomination

1988 Jackson makes second unsuccessful bid for nomination

1992 Acquittal of four police officers accused of beating suspect Rodney King sparks race riots in Los Angeles leaving 53 people dead

2005 Hurricane Katrina devastates New Orleans, killing 1,836 people

2008 Barack Obama wins presidential election

2009 **20 January:** Obama inaugurated as 44th president

Further reading

Taylor Branch, *America in the King Years* (Simon and Schuster 2006)

Taylor Branch's three books on Martin Luther King and the civil rights movement in the period 1954–68 have received well-deserved praise and critical acclaim. Taylor Branch covers all aspects of King's life and the civil rights years in exhaustive detail. In the final pages of his last book in the trilogy, *At Canaan's Edge*, the author attempts to summarise the extraordinary legacy of Martin Luther King. On p. 770 he writes:

> Statecraft is still preoccupied with the levers of spies and force, even though two centuries of increasingly lethal 'total warfare' since Napoleon suggest a diminishing power of violence to sustain governance in the modern world. Military leaders themselves often stress the political limits of warfare, but politics is slow to recognise the glaring impact of nonviolent power…King himself upheld nonviolence until he was nearly alone among colleagues weary of sacrifice. To the end he resisted incitements to violence, cynicism and tribal retreat. He grasped freedom seen and unseen, rooted in ecumenical faith, sustaining patriotism to brighten the heritage of his country for all people. These treasures abide with lasting promise from America in the King years.

Hugh Brogan, *The Penguin History of the USA* (Penguin 2001)

It is difficult to understand the civil rights movement without a good general knowledge of American history. Hugh Brogan manages to achieve the rare feat of writing a general history that is both informative and enjoyable to read. Here (p. 615) he describes the South in the early part of the twentieth century, making it clear why blacks would have to fight so hard for an end to segregation:

> The bland smile of American democracy displayed a rotten tooth, or rather two rotten teeth. The plight of the South and that of the African-Americans. They were and always had been intimately related, never more so than at the beginning of the twentieth century, when 85% of the 8,800,000 African-Americans lived in the South, a region where the per capita income was little more than half the national average…Before the First World War the final touches were put to the Jim Crow edifice, and in spite of all the brave aspirations to a 'New South' the region stood supreme in disease, poverty, ignorance, sloth, hunger and cruelty.

Adam Fairclough, *Better Day Coming: Blacks and Equality, 1890–2000* (Penguin 2001)

Adam Fairclough's readable book is a comprehensive account of the civil rights movement in America over the last century. On p. 304 he summarises the appeal and achievements of Malcolm X, one of the movement's most controversial figures:

> Malcolm X had been murdered six months before the Watts riot, gunned down by members of the Nation of Islam at the age of thirty nine...In the early 1960s Malcolm X had represented an ideological counterforce to the civil rights movement — one that was often invoked by civil rights leaders themselves for the purposes of frightening white elites. After his death Malcolm became a heroic symbol both to advocates of violence and proponents of Black Nationalism. In the Northern ghettos, Malcolm, dead, often seemed more influential than King, alive.

Juan Williams, *Eyes on the Prize: America's Civil Rights Years, 1954–65* (Penguin 1987)

This is the companion book for the American Public Broadcasting Service's epic documentary series on the civil rights movement entitled *Eyes on the Prize*. On p. 249 a young black woman called Fannie Lou Hamer present in Mississippi during Freedom Summer remembers the impact of that time:

> There was no real civil rights movement in the Negro community in Mississippi before the 1964 Summer Project. There were people who wanted change, but they hadn't dared to come out and try to do something, to try to change the way things were. But after the 1964 project when all of the young people came down for the summer — an exciting and remarkable summer — Negro people in the delta began moving. People who had never before tried, though they had always been anxious to do something, began moving...To see kids, to see these people — to see how far they'd come since 1964! To me it's one of the greatest things that ever happened in Mississippi. And it's a direct result of the Summer 1964 project.

Gary Younge, *Stranger in a Strange land — Encounters in the Disunited States* (The New Press 2006) and *No Place Like Home* (Picador 1999)

Gary Younge is a black British-born *Guardian* journalist living in America. He has established himself as one of the foremost contemporary commentators on civil rights. His writing is accessible, perceptive and very readable, and these two books are full of succinct observations about the state of race relations (and many other matters) in America today. An extract from *Stranger in a Strange Land* (p. 119) on the paradox of America demonstrates his writing talent:

America was built on discrimination. From the theft of the land from the Native Americans to the theft of labour during slavery; from Uncle Tom's Cabin in the nineteenth century to the shacks that house migrant Mexican workers in the twenty-first. But it was also built on an ideal, that 'all men were created equal' and free in 'their pursuit of life, liberty and happiness'. It is a principle that continues to attract millions of immigrants to the country and inspire the citizens within it. These two competing traditions are what make America what it is today. Without the discrimination it would not be so powerful, wealthy or racially and ethnically balkanised. Without the ideal it would not be so dynamic, hopeful, confident and culturally vibrant.

Glossary

abolitionist

A term used to describe someone supporting the abolition of slavery before the American Civil War. The abolitionist movement became powerful globally in the 1800s and led to the abolition of slavery by the British Empire and other countries. America ended slavery after the Civil War.

accommodation

The efforts by African-Americans in the South to come to terms with the segregated system and to work within it to improve their living standards. Its most famous proponent was Booker T. Washington, who set up the Tuskegee Institute to teach blacks in the South various practical 'trades' so that they could earn a decent living. The philosophy of accommodation was criticised for accepting segregation.

activist

A person involved in political campaigning on a particular issue or for a particular party. Activists tend to show more commitment to a cause than others and are crucial to a party or campaign's successes.

African-American

The term used to describe Americans of African decent. They may have origins in any of the black populations of Africa. Most African-Americans are direct descendants of captive Africans who survived the slavery era, although some are descended from voluntary immigrants.

apartheid

A system of government practised by South Africa between 1948 and 1990 that strictly separated society on a racial basis and gave privileged positions to the white population. The whites of both British and Boer or Afrikaans descent benefited from this system. Apartheid legally instituted racism and stripped blacks of their citizenship rights.

Black Nationalism

A movement that encouraged African-Americans to take pride in their racial origins and to resist attempts by whites to portray them as inferior. It also urged them to resist racial oppression and stand up for themselves. It was linked to other movements such as Black Power and 'Back to Africa'.

Black Panther Party (Black Panthers)

An organisation set up in 1966 by Bobby Seale and Huey Newton, an SNCC veteran.

boycott

The practice of refusing to buy from, use or deal with a particular company or commercial organisation. It is a form of consumer activism usually carried out for political reasons.

Brotherhood of Sleeping Car Porters (BSCP)

A trade union led by African-Americans, with black members. In the 1920s it hired Philip Randolph to lead a successful strike for better conditions in one of the first mass actions by blacks.

Citizens' Councils

Groups set up throughout the South to resist integration and support segregation. They consisted of local whites and often had links to law enforcement agencies and the Ku Klux Klan. Although supposedly law-abiding, they were often involved in fomenting racial hatred and violence against civil rights activists and blacks.

civil rights

The concept that people have 'civil rights' is a relatively new one, which has become widespread only since the eighteenth century. The USA was one of the first countries to recognise people had 'rights', and protected them in its constitution. Civil rights include, for example, the right to participate in government, the rights of freedom of expression, assembly and travel, as well as freedom from the abuse of government power. The US Constitution promised such rights to all its citizens but effectively denied them to many, such as black slaves, Native Americans and women.

Cold War

The state of tension and conflict between the USA and the Union of Soviet Socialist Republics (the USSR) between 1945 and 1990.

Communist Party of the USA (CPUSA)

In the 1930s this was almost the only white-dominated organisation to advocate integration, but it was discredited by its association with Stalin in the post-1945 Cold War.

Congress of Racial Equality (CORE)

This civil rights organisation, founded in 1942 in Chicago by a group of students including Bayard Rustin, Bernice Fisher and James Farmer, was dedicated to non-violence and direct action.

Constitution of the USA

This document, signed after the United States' War of Independence by the states that had successfully broken away from Britain, forms the basis of the system of government that still operates in America. A number of Amendments have subsequently been added to it. These Amendments include a Bill of Rights and the abolition of slavery.

Council of Federated Organizations (COFO)

An organisation formed in 1962 to coordinate the actions of civil rights organisations in Mississippi and concerned with increasing voter registration in the state.

direct action

The policy of active confrontation adopted by the civil rights movement from the mid-1950s onwards. It included passive resistance, non-cooperation, accepting arrest and demonstrating against segregation. Direct action campaigns in southern cities focused the world's media on the issue of civil rights and helped pressurise the federal government into taking action.

Dixiecrat

A southern Democrat committed to segregation. Derived from Dixie, nickname for the southern states of America, referring to the 11 southern states that tried to leave the USA in the Civil War.

Emancipation

During the Civil War Abraham Lincoln passed two Emancipation Proclamations that promised to free slaves in the southern states opposing the Unionist forces. In 1865 the Thirteenth Amendment abolished slavery throughout the USA.

federal government

The USA has a federal system of government. The country is decentralised, with major powers in areas such as taxation and education given to state governments, but with a central, federal government whose laws take precedence, at least in theory, over state laws.

Fellowship of Reconciliation (FOR)

An organisation set up to train civil rights activists in non-violence and protest.

freedom rides

The practice adopted by black and white activists of travelling by federal buses through the segregated South and refusing to sit in segregated parts of the buses. The tactic was first adopted by CORE in the 1940s and was used again in the 1960s.

hippy

> The hippy movement was originally a youth subculture that started in the USA in the 1960s and spread across the world. The word, derived from *hipster* and from the beatnik movement of the 1950s, is a loose term that can be used to describe a variety of different groups and behaviours. Their links with the civil rights movement were vague, but their emphasis on individual freedoms and peaceful protest against the Vietnam War provided some common ground.

integration

> The segregation of whites and blacks in the South of the USA would only be ended by their integration, which meant blacks and whites would attend the same schools, use the same shops, sit in the same areas on public transport and be offered the same opportunities regardless of race.

Jim Crow

> The segregated system instituted in the South after the Civil War that denied blacks equal rights. The origin of the term is obscure. 'Jim Crow' laws were those that limited black opportunities in (among other areas) education, employment and voting.

Ku Klux Klan

> The Ku Klux Klan originated in the aftermath of the Civil War and was founded in 1865 by former Confederate army soldiers. It soon grew into a secretive and militant terrorist organisation consisting of white supremacists who wanted to maintain segregation and intimidate blacks into accepting the racist status quo in the South. It was repressed in 1870–71 but revived in 1915 in the North and gained up to 5 million supporters. It was anti-Semitic, anti-Catholic, anti-immigrant and anti-black. It declined in popularity in the 1930s but retained a residual support in the South, and was responsible for many acts of violence in the civil rights era. Its name comes from the Greek *kuklos*, meaning a circle.

lynching

> Extra-judicial killing of suspects in the USA, once a widespread practice. It originally developed as a form of 'frontier justice' when law enforcement was scarce and local communities dealt with criminals as they saw fit. However, in many states of America it continued into the twentieth century and most of the victims were black men. Hundreds of blacks were murdered by mobs of angry whites, often with little or no evidence of guilt.

March on Washington Movement (MOWM)

> This was founded in 1941 after the threatened March on Washington by Philip Randolph.

minister

In Christian churches the minister is the spiritual leader, authorised to conduct services, weddings, baptisms and funerals. In the South of the USA ministers played a very important role in the black community — they were often in effect community leaders in a society that denied blacks most other opportunities.

Mississippi Freedom Democratic Party (MFDP)

Set up by civil rights groups operating in Mississippi, this organisation challenged the Democratic Party internally. It sent delegations to the Democratic convention in 1964 but Lyndon Johnson refused to recognise them as official party representatives.

Montgomery Improvement Association (MIA)

An organisation founded in December 1955 with Martin Luther King as president, with the purpose of organising the bus boycott in Montgomery.

National Aeronautics and Space Administration (NASA)

A federal agency established in 1958 to challenge the Soviet lead in what became the 'space race'. Many of its key functions, such as the principal launch site at Cape Canaveral and Mission Control in Houston, were integrated establishments deliberately sited in the South.

National Alliance of Postal Employees (NAPE)

Founded in 1913, this was the first all-black trade union.

National Association for the Advancement of Colored People (NAACP)

Set up in 1909 (emerging from the Niagara movement of 1905), its chief figure was W. E. B. Du Bois. Its main tactic was litigation against segregation. After 1917 it had a new secretary, James Weldon Johnson. It also had a newspaper, the *Crisis*, of which Du Bois was editor. The *Crisis* was linked to the NAACP but enjoyed more widespread popularity. The NAACP also had a Youth Council.

National Association of Colored Women (NACW)

Founded in 1896, by 1900 this had 18,000 women members in 300 local clubs. It was essentially a conservative organisation aimed at helping black women to achieve moderate reforms and highlight various causes. However, it was effective in its campaign against lynching.

Nation of Islam

A movement founded in 1930. Its most famous member was Malcolm X, who set up the Organization of Afro-American Unity.

Native American

A term used to describe the indigenous peoples from the regions of North America now encompassed by the USA and Canada. They comprised a large number of distinct tribes (many subsequently wiped out by European settlers). They have also been called by other names, such as American Indians, Red Indians and Aboriginal Indians.

non-violence

The practice of refusing to retaliate to the use of physical force. Non-violence had been practised successfully by the Indian leader Mahatma Gandhi against the British in the Indian struggle for independence. Civil rights leaders in America adopted it as their primary tactic in the 1950s and 1960s, although divisions over its effectiveness meant that by 1965 some had abandoned it.

the North

The North, or the northern states of America, traditionally refers to the states that opposed those states that tried to secede from the USA in the Civil War. In the context of this book it is also used in a more general way to refer to any northern states outside the segregationist South.

People United to Serve Humanity (PUSH)

A civil rights organisation set up be Rev. Jesse Jackson and based in Chicago. It is linked to the Rainbow Coalition and has worked to improve the conditions for blacks but also as a platform for Jesse Jackson's political ambitions.

plantation

The type of farming used to cultivate crops such as tobacco and sugar cane. Large farms were needed, where labour was intensive and extremely hard. Plantation farmers supported the use of slaves in the eighteenth and nineteenth centuries, as it allowed them to maximise profits while minimising labour costs.

quotas

The practice of assigning a certain percentage of places in an institution or company to certain groups of people. Generally they are used as part of an affirmative action programme and often apply to black applicants to college.

Rainbow Coalition

An organisation founded by the Rev. Jesse Jackson in 1984 to help pursue social justice for black people. It merged with PUSH in 1996.

reconstruction

The process after the Civil War whereby the North tried to push through reforms in the South to end segregation and integrate white and blacks. Congress approved the military occupation of the South and the passing of the Fourteenth and Fifteenth Amendments, but failed to end segregation and by the 1890s had abandoned the attempt.

segregation

The system in the South of the USA that separated people according to their race. Designed to prevent blacks achieving equality in the aftermath of the Civil War, segregation denied them equal access to education, housing, employment, justice, public transport and most importantly the right to vote. It was this system that civil rights activists challenged in the 1950s and 1960s

sit-in

The tactic adopted by civil rights activists of entering a restaurant or lunch counter in department stores such as Woolworth's and refusing to sit in the segregated areas. Adopted as a widespread tactic in 1960, the sit-in movement spread across the segregated South and led to widespread civil unrest as many were arrested and mobs attacked the activists. It was an effective way of challenging segregation and helped to end it.

slavery

Slavery in the USA began soon after the first colonists arrived and settled Virginia in 1607. It lasted until 1865 and the passage of the Thirteenth Amendment. Africans captured or bought by slave traders in Africa were sold to Europeans who transported them to South and North America and the 'Sugar Islands' of the Caribbean. Slaves were sold in North America and were effectively the property of their owners.

the South

Traditionally, 'the South' refers to the Confederate states, the 11 states that attempted to leave the USA (and failed) in the American Civil War. Some or all of the additional seven states that had slavery but did not fight for the Confederacy, such as Kentucky and Maryland, could also be regarded as part of this group. During the civil rights period it might be more useful to think of 'the South' in a narrower sense, in terms of the most segregated states and those that saw major campaigns: Virginia, the Carolinas, Georgia, Alabama, Mississippi, Louisiana, Tennessee and Arkansas.

Southern Christian Leadership Conference (SCLC)

The SCLC, set up in January 1957, was an indigenous southern movement that differed from the NAACP by virtue of being very religious. It got help from northern advisors such as Bayard Rustin and tended to focus on mass action (and so was often critical of the NAACP).

Student Nonviolent Coordinating Committee (SNCC)

Formed in April 1960, this represented an attempt by a new generation of civil rights campaigners to redefine the civil rights struggle. The SCLC's Ella Baker was a key figure in setting it up (she had become disillusioned with Martin Luther King and wanted a more democratic organisation). The SNCC was southern, black and radical. Like the SCLC it believed in confrontation and direct action. Its relations with the NAACP were often strained and from 1961 it was focused on Mississippi. It helped create the Council of Federated Organizations (COFO) with other civil rights groups to register voters. After 1964 it became increasingly attracted to the Black Power movement and in the 1970s it fell apart.

Uncle Tom

A derogatory term used to describe blacks seen as overly subservient to or co-operative with the white power structure in America. The term originates from the novel *Uncle Tom's Cabin* by Harriet Beecher Stowe, published in 1852. The book actually criticised slavery, but the central character Tom remained too subservient for many later African-Americans and he has become a byword for blacks who are over-eager to please white people.

Unionist

The term used to describe the armies that fought for the North in the Civil War against the Confederate forces. They were called Unionist forces, as they supported the Union (the USA).

Universal Negro Improvement Association (UNIA)

An organisation founded in 1916–17 by Marcus Garvey and based in New York. It was an early Black Nationalist organisation that encouraged black pride and a focus on Africa as the cradle of civilisation.

PHILIP ALLAN
UPDATES

Student Unit Guides

There are guides to help you in the following subjects:

Accounting (AQA)

Biology (AQA, Edexcel, OCR)

Business Studies (AQA, Edexcel, OCR)

Chemistry (AQA, Edexcel, OCR (A), OCR (B) (Salters))

Economics (AQA, Edexcel, OCR)

English Language (AQA)

English Language and Literature (AQA)

Geography (AQA, Edexcel, OCR)

Government & Politics (AQA, Edexcel, OCR)

History (Edexcel, OCR)

Law (AQA, OCR)

Mathematics (AQA, Edexcel, OCR)

Media Studies (AQA, OCR)

Physical Education (AQA, Edexcel, OCR)

Physics (Edexcel, OCR)

Psychology (AQA (A), AQA (B), Edexcel, OCR)

Sociology (AQA, OCR)

- Focus your revision
- Build your confidence
- Strengthen your exam technique

Visit **www.philipallan.co.uk** for the full list of unit guides and to order online, or telephone our Customer Services Department on **01235 827720**